Easy Guide to

FIVE-CARD MAJORS

Sally Brock

First published 2004

© Sally Brock 2004

The right of Sally Brock to be identified as Author of this work has been asserted by her in accordance with the Copyright, Designs and Patents Act 1988.

ISBN 0 7134 8912 X

A CIP catalogue record for this book is available from the British Library.

Typeset in the U.K. by Wakewing, High Wycombe
Printed in the U.K. by Creative Print & Design, Ebbw Vale, Wales

for the publishers

B T Batsford, The Chrysalis Building, Bramley Road, London W10 6SP

An imprint of **Chrysalis** Books Group

Distributed in the United States and Canada by Sterling Publishing Co., 387 Park Avenue South, New York, NY 10016, USA

Editor: Elena Jeronimidis

CONTENTS

INTRODUCTION

The Acol bidding system was invented in London in about 1934, though it has been constantly evolving ever since. It is the most widely played system in Great Britain and some of its colonies but it never really caught on worldwide. The world in general prefers to play five-card majors, as opposed to the four-card Acol variety.

For many years British club and tournament players have largely been faithful to their Acol methods but times are changing. There are more and more international bridge events open to ordinary players, and the cost of international travel has reduced significantly. All this means that more people are travelling further afield to play their favourite game, which inevitably means an increased interest in 'foreign' bidding methods. Even if players intend to stay loyal to Acol, it is important to learn about what the rest of the world plays, if only to understand fully what is going on.

This book is aimed at the experienced club or tournament player who has been playing Acol for years but who is interested in learning about five-card majors, perhaps to play the 'new' system himself, or maybe just to understand its ramifications better.

Just as there is much variation in the minutiae of Acol, so there is in the five-card major world. When proposing a particular treatment I have tried to put both sides of the argument, so the reader can make up his own mind precisely as to which method to adopt. When giving example hands I have tried not to make everything too clear-cut. In real life bidding decisions are often complex; there is no perfect bid and we simply have to do the best we can to describe our hand as closely as possible, i.e. to choose the lesser of several evils. Because of this some may disagree with my suggested action on some of the example hands. That is fine with me. What I am trying to get across is where the problem lies and the pros and cons of the alternative solutions. I do not apologise for any personal bias in some of the recommended sequences.

The book is illustrated with many examples and each section ends with quizzes to test the reader's understanding. In addition, at the end of each 'part' is a 'What Went Wrong?' quiz where the reader is invited to decide exactly that.

By the time the reader reaches the end of the book he should be perfectly well equipped to play his new bidding system at any club or tournament in the world.

In closing, I would like to thank everyone who has helped me with this book: Elena Jeronimidis, Barry Rigal, the ACBL for permission to quote from *The Official Encyclopedia of Bridge,* and last but by no means least, my husband, Raymond.

Sally Brock
June 2004

SETTING THE SCENE

It is not really possible to write a book about five-card majors without also establishing a no-trump range. Although by no means universal, four-card majors are usually played with a weak no-trump, while five-card majors tend to be allied to a strong no-trump. When I give example hands and present quizzes to test readers' understanding I need to make assumptions about that no-trump range.

Perhaps this book would have been better entitled *Five-card Majors, Strong No-trump* for that is its subject matter. In addition, there is the issue of precisely what strength a strong no-trump should be. I would like to arrive at an answer to that question in rather a round-about way . . . A weak balanced hand, i.e. a standard weak no-trump, is the most frequent opening bid. It is important that you have good definition in these mamma-poppa sequences. In my view if you open one of a suit, when you rebid 1NT you should have only a 3 HCP range, i.e. it should be 11–13, 12–14 or 13–15. Some people like to open 11-counts but in my view an 11–14 1NT rebid is too wide a range. Partner has to invite game with a decent 11 points opposite, but (a) sometimes gets too high facing 11, and (b) sometimes gets too high when partner presses on with a decent 12-count 'because he might have had 11'. If you want to open 11-counts (and this includes me) – and by that I mean real 11-counts, not 11-counts that are so good they are really worth 12-counts – then you should play a 14–16 no-trump; if you are happy to pass most 11-counts, then play a 15–17 no-trump. Only if you are really happy to pass most 12-counts should you consider playing a 16–18 no-trump (but you'll be missing out on a lot of fun).

In this book we will take the middle course and play, along with most of the world, a 15–17 no-trump.

The aim is to present a cohesive system which fits together well. In *Part III Clever Stuff*, I look at some of the more common conventions which work well with five-card major, strong no-trump methods. Although these conventions are commonplace in the United States, they are less well-known in Britain, simply because they do not fit in well with the four-card major, 12–14 no-trump, Acol style.

For example, it is not possible to play game-forcing Two-over-One bids with Acol. Acol players needs to be able to pass a 1NT response when they have 15–16 points and a balanced hand. If an Acol player wishes to be in game facing a balanced hand with 15–16 points, i.e. he has a decent 9-count or thereabouts, he needs to respond at the two level or game will be missed on a regular basis.

If, on the other hand, partner will already have opened 1NT with this 15–16 point hand, then it is a different matter entirely. A 1NT response can be made comfortably with 10 or a poor 11 points, because the only time (more or less) opener will want to pass 1NT is when he has 12–14 points and a 5-3-3-2 distribution in which case 1NT is likely to be the right contract.

A sound intermediate-level bidding system is the end product, one which stands well as it is, or acts as a good base on which partnerships can add their own individual flourishes.

One final point: this book assumes that the reader is familiar with Roman Key Card Blackwood (RKCB), which is the most common slam convention in use in the tournament world. As with ordinary Blackwood, 4NT asks for aces, but in RKCB the king of trumps is included as an extra ace. The responses are: 5♣ = 0 or 3, 5◊ = 1 or 4, 5♡ = 2, 5♠ = 2 plus the queen of trumps. After a 5♣ or 5◊ response, the next step up (which is not the agreed trump suit) asks for the queen of trumps – without it responder bids the next step, with it responder shows some previously undisclosed high card or else goes back to the agreed trump suit.

PART I
OPENING WITH A FIVE-CARD MAJOR

What to Open?

You may think this is self-evident. Perhaps you think that if you have a five-card major you should always open it. Generally that is so but there are certainly exceptions.

A Five-card Major and a Six-card Minor

Once upon a time I held a hand of 1-5-6-1 distribution. I can no longer remember the precise hand but I had about a 12-count and my suits were roughly equal in terms of strength. I opened 1♡. The next hand overcalled 1♠ and my partner bid 1NT. My right-hand opponent bid 2♠ and I rebid 3◊. Now my left-hand opponent bid 3♠ which was passed round to me. I pressed on with 4◊, my partner returned to 4♡ and this was doubled by my right-hand opponent. This was the whole sequence:

West	North	East	South
1♡	1♠	1NT	2♠
3◊	3♠	Pass	Pass
4◊	Pass	4♡	Dble
All Pass			

I was a little unlucky, as the hand who had overcalled 1♠ had *six* hearts. I went for 1400 in 4♡ doubled when the opponents needed to find their heart ruff to beat 5◊.

This board occurred in an international event in 1980 and it is the last time I opened a five-card major when I had a six-card minor.

I would be the first to acknowledge that many expert bridge players have not had this experience and feel less strongly than I do about this, some even preferring to open their major.

One reason I feel that it often works out badly to bid your suits the wrong way round is that when you are distributional then usually the opponents are too. Before you know it the bidding escalates to some high level and it is imperative that you find your best fit. If you have bid your shorter suit first partner will tend to keep putting you back to it when he has equal length. The difference between a 6-3 fit and a 5-3 fit at the five level when suits are breaking badly and the opponents are punching you can be considerable.

The proponents of the 'major first' brigade may argue that it is often difficult to introduce your second suit into the auction at all when the bidding takes off. Maybe that used to be true but in these days of negative doubles and other modern gadgets it is much easier.

Suppose you hold:

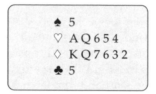

You open 1◇ and your left-hand opponent overcalls 1♠. Most of the time when partner has four hearts he will double. If he doubles you know the sky's the limit. But suppose he bids 2♣, and the next hand bids 4♠. Now you can bid 4NT. This is a two-suited take-out bid. You may make it with some club support and a good diamond suit, or a hand such as the one here. If partner bids the expected 5♣ you bid 5◇ and partner knows that you have a five-card heart suit too. It must be a five-card suit because you would never expect him to have a four-card heart suit when he does not double 1♠. But suppose he has a hand such as:

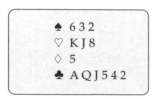

He can convert to 5♡. You may have done the wrong thing by bidding at all, but at least you should end up in your best spot.

A Strong No-trump with a Five-card Major

If you are dealt a balanced hand with 15–17 points and a five-card major there are two alternative styles:

- **The French style**
  The French open one of their five-card suit and if their partner responds at the two level they rebid 2NT, forcing to game with 15+ points. This part of the system will be familiar to weak no-trumpers and if you are changing over from a standard weak no-trump four-card-major Acol base, this may be the style you choose. If you have a balanced hand in the 12–14 range with a five-card major then you have to rebid it. Again, this is a familiar style to Acolites.

- **The American style**
  The Americans open 1NT with 15–17 points and a balanced hand, regardless of whether or not they hold a five-card major. If they open one of a major and rebid 2NT over a two-level response this shows 12–14 points. The upside for them is that if they rebid their suit they have an unbalanced hand, usually with six in the suit opened (but sometimes they are stuck with a 5-4-3-1 where the order of the suits is such that they cannot show their second suit).

I prefer the American style and that is what you should assume in this book. I am deeply wedded to the idea that if you have a balanced hand you should open or rebid no-trumps. I do not like having to open one of a suit and rebid two with a 5-3-3-2 distribution. As we will see later, the Americans can happily respond 1NT to one of a major with a 10-count, knowing that partner will only pass with a balanced hand in the 12–14 range. (Indeed, many Americans like to play a two-level response as game-forcing, in which case they either play a forcing 1NT response, or at least allow it to be up to 11 points. The French, on the other hand, respond in a similar style to Acol, needing to go to the two level with about 9 points. And, as in Acol, sometimes this results in a rather silly 5-1 fit.)

If you are going to open 1NT regularly with a five-card major then you should consider adopting Puppet Stayman in place of the more normal variety.

Puppet Stayman

Using Puppet Stayman, 2♣ asks in the first instance for a five-card major not a four-carder. In its simple version, a 2◇ response denies, while two of a major promises a five-carder. After the 2◇ denial, responder can introduce a four-card major which shows at least invitational values, and the 4-4 fit can then be found.

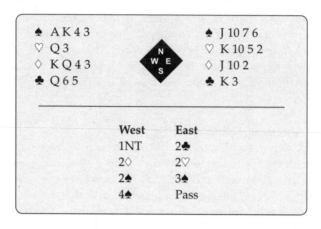

	♠ A K 4 3		♠ J 10 7 6
	♡ Q 3		♡ K 10 5 2
	◇ K Q 4 3		◇ J 10 2
	♣ Q 6 5		♣ K 3

West	East
1NT	2♣
2◇	2♡
2♠	3♠
4♠	Pass

West's 2◇ denies a five-card major. East's 2♡ shows a four-card suit and is forcing for one round, showing at least invitational values. West shows his four-card spade suit, East makes an invitational raise and West presses on to game. East and West have both been pushy but the modern style is to reach thin games. Had they been playing normal Stayman, the bidding would have gone 1NT – 2♣ – 2♠ – 3♠ – 4♠. The information exchanged is similar and the judgement would be the same.

Actually the Puppet Stayman sequence has been more revealing, both to East-West and North-South. As East has four hearts his minor-suit doubleton is likely to be useful and this knowledge might just tip the balance in West's decision as to whether or not to raise to game.

What would you open on the following hands?

(1)
- ♠ A K Q 6 5
- ♡ 5 4
- ◇ —
- ♣ J 9 8 5 4 2

(2)
- ♠ A Q 6 5 3
- ♡ J 5 4
- ◇ A 6
- ♣ K J 7

(3)
- ♠ Q 3
- ♡ A Q J 5
- ◇ K 8 7 3 2
- ♣ A 10

(4)
- ♠ 8
- ♡ A
- ◇ K Q 10 3 2
- ♣ K 9 8 5 3 2

(5)
- ♠ A K 10 6 5
- ♡ A K 2
- ◇ 3 2
- ♣ K 5 4

(6)
- ♠ 8 2
- ♡ A K 5 4
- ◇ A Q 10 7 6
- ♣ K 2

(7)
- ♠ 10
- ♡ A K Q J 3
- ◇ 10 9 8 4 3 2
- ♣ A

(8)
- ♠ K 5
- ♡ Q 6 4 3 2
- ◇ K J 10 2
- ♣ A Q

(9)
- ♠ 7 6
- ♡ A K 10 5 4
- ◇ A Q 3 2
- ♣ K 3

(10)
- ♠ A K 8 7 3
- ♡ A Q 10 8 7 2
- ◇ 4
- ♣ 8

(11)
- ♠ K 5
- ♡ J 4
- ◇ A Q J 10 7 6
- ♣ A J 3

(12)
- ♠ K 5
- ♡ J 4
- ◇ A Q J 10 7 6
- ♣ Q J 6

(13)
- ♠ Q J 10 6 5
- ♡ A
- ◇ K Q J 6 5 4
- ♣ 8

(14)
- ♠ K 5
- ♡ J 4
- ◇ K J 7 6 3 2
- ♣ A K 2

(15)
- ♠ J 10 4 3
- ♡ K Q 4 3
- ◇ A K 9 3
- ♣ K

What would you open on the following hands?

(1)	(2)	(3)
♠ A K Q 6 5	♠ A Q 6 5 3	♠ Q 3
♡ 5 4	♡ J 5 4	♡ A Q J 5
◊ —	◊ A 6	◊ K 8 7 3 2
♣ J 9 8 5 4 2	♣ K J 7	♣ A 10

(1) Even with very poor clubs and good spades it is much more convenient to open 1♣ and later rebid spades.

(2) With honours in every suit open 1NT despite the five-card major.

(3) Don't let the 5-4 distribution put you off, especially when your four-card suit is higher ranking than the five-carder. Again, with honours in all your suits open 1NT. Although you are just strong enough to reverse, the auction will be more straightforward if you open 1NT.

(4)	(5)	(6)
♠ 8	♠ A K 10 6 5	♠ 8 2
♡ A	♡ A K 2	♡ A K 5 4
◊ K Q 10 3 2	◊ 3 2	◊ A Q 10 7 6
♣ K 9 8 5 3 2	♣ K 5 4	♣ K 2

(4) Although in some ways it would be more convenient to open 1◊, if the opponents come into the auction, as seems likely, it may be important to play in your longer minor at the five level. I recommend opening 1♣.

(5) With excellent controls and a five-card suit, this is too good to open 1NT. Open 1♠ instead.

(6) This hand also looks better for suit play. You have the values for a reverse, so open 1◊, intending to rebid 2♡ on the next round.

(7)	(8)	(9)
♠ 10	♠ K 5	♠ 7 6
♡ A K Q J 3	♡ Q 6 4 3 2	♡ A K 10 5 4
◇ 10 9 8 4 3 2	◇ K J 10 2	◇ A Q 3 2
♣ A	♣ A Q	♣ K 3

(7) This one could almost tempt me, but I will stay true to my principles and still open 1◇, though I have to say that most experts would prefer 1♡.

(8) Open 1NT. Despite the 5-4 distribution and convenient suits to bid, this still looks more like a no-trump hand to me because of the strong doubletons and the weak heart suit. In addition, it looks like a hand where I would rather be declarer because of my black-suit holdings.

(9) On the other hand, this one, with more aces, good hearts and a weak doubleton, is much more suitable for play in a suit contract. Open 1♡.

(10)	(11)	(12)
♠ A K 8 7 3	♠ K 5	♠ K 5
♡ A Q 10 8 7 2	♡ J 4	♡ J 4
◇ 4	◇ A Q J 10 7 6	◇ A Q J 10 7 6
♣ 8	♣ A J 3	♣ Q J 6

(10) Although you have only 13 high-card points, with two decent suits this hand is really promising. Open 1♡, intending to reverse into spades on the next round.

(11) Some people like to open 1NT with this type of hand but in my opinion the six-card suit makes it too strong. Open 1◇ and rebid 2NT if partner responds in a major.

(12) Here the sixth diamond makes the hand worth a 1NT opening.

(13)	**(14)**	**(15)**
♠ Q J 10 6 5	♠ K 5	♠ J 10 4 3
♡ A	♡ J 4	♡ K Q 4 3
◊ K Q J 6 5 4	◊ K J 7 6 3 2	◊ A K 9 3
♣ 8	♣ A K 2	♣ K

(13) Again, no reason to distort your hand. Open 1◊.

(14) Here when the suit is weak, the 1NT opening is fine.

(15) Although no-one likes to open 1NT with a singleton, when the singleton is a minor and an honour to boot, it is surely the best alternative.

WHAT HAVE WE LEARNED?

A   When you are 6-5, open your longest suit even if it is the lower ranking. If your second suit is spades you will be able to introduce it easily enough, while if the opponents have spades and bounce the auction it is important to be able to play in your best fit.

B   With 15–17 points and your values spread evenly around your hand (or in your short suits), open 1NT even with a five-card major or a 5-4-2-2 distribution. But with more concentrated values open your long suit.

C   Don't open 1NT when you are in range *and* have a good six-card minor. That makes your hand too strong. But when you are a little light in points, that sixth card can make the hand worth an opening 1NT. Don't forget that the point-count system is only a guide, not a rule to be followed slavishly.

Differences in Responding Strategy

When I first started to play serious bridge I thought the idea of bidding was to have long scientific auctions to reach the right contract. I no longer think that's what it is all about. Now if I can see what is likely to be the right contract, I bid it and hope to give away as little information about my hand as possible. Long auctions help opponents with the opening lead and the defence in general. I don't know if anyone has conducted a proper statistical survey, but I would be prepared to bet a large amount of money that at game level the longer the auction the less chance there is of success.

When opener holds a five-card major life is wonderful. We can often have a short auction to the top spot without needing to give away information to the opposition. (Four-card major enthusiasts will argue that while this is true when opener has a five-card major the opposite is true when he does not.) If the fit is found immediately responder can raise. If responder has less than three-card support and responds 1NT opener knows there is no support and doesn't have to waste another round of bidding looking for it.

Even when partner opens 1♡ and you hold three-card support but also a spade suit, there is no need to do other than raise hearts when you have a weak hand. With four spades and three hearts always raise to 2♡; with five spades and three hearts you should generally also raise to 2♡ unless the spades are very strong. No longer will you have those nightmare auctions you had when you played four-card majors and you responded 1♠ on a four-card suit and partner raised to 2♠. You had to struggle with a trump suit of J-x-x-x facing K-x-x when you had a perfectly good 5-3 heart fit.

Even when responder has four or more cards in support his life is easier when he knows there is a five-card suit opposite. That extra card opposite makes it safer for him to bid to a higher level himself. It is rarely wrong to bid to the three level with a nine-card fit but it can often be wrong to do so when the fit is only eight cards.

Let's take a look at some deals and compare the five-card and four-card major auctions.

♠ A K 9 6 5	♠ Q 10 7
♡ A	♡ K 10 4 3
◇ A Q 10 9 4	◇ 8 7 3
♣ 7 6	♣ K 8 2

Five-card major auction:

West	East
1♠	2♠
4♠	pass

West knows of the 5-3 spade fit, so there is no purpose in doing anything other than bidding game directly. It is extremely unlikely that 4♠ is not the right game, and there is no real likelihood that slam can be on.

Four-card major auction:

West	East
1♠	1NT
3◇	4♠
pass	

With a 4-3-3-3 distribution it is normal for East to respond 1NT. Now West does not know of the three-card support and has to check for it. If partner has fewer than three spades 5◇ or even 6◇ might be on. For instance, partner may hold:

♠ 7 2
♡ 9 8 2
◇ K J 6 5 2
♣ A 8 5

So West bids 3◇, revealing more of his hand. Maybe the five-card major auction would attract a diamond lead. The four-card major auction certainly would not.

Five-card major auction:

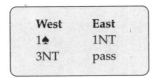

West	East
1♠	1NT
3NT	pass

As soon as West knows that his partner does not have three-card spade support, it is clear to bid the no-trump game directly. Hopefully he will avoid a club lead, but even on a club lead nine tricks are likely.

Four-card major auction:

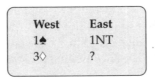

West	East
1♠	1NT
3◊	?

Now East has a tricky bid to find. Should he just close his eyes and bid 3NT, or should he worry that he has nothing in clubs? He is probably best to bid 3♡. At IMP scoring it does not matter very much what West does now but at match-point scoring he no longer has a winning option: he can either bid the lower-scoring spade game or play in 3NT on a likely club lead.

♠ A K Q J 6		♠ 10 3
♡ 4		♡ 9 7 3
◊ A 10 9 5 2		◊ K Q 4
♣ A 3		♣ K 8 7 5 2

Five-card major auction:

West	East
1♠	1NT
3◊	3♠
4◊	5◊
6◊	pass

East knows that West has not bid 3◊ on any old hand just to discover if he has three-card spade support. West is making a strong suggestion that no-trumps might not be the best denomination. It would be unthinkable for East to bid 3NT with nothing in hearts (with his hearts and clubs reversed he would bid 3♡). East marks time with 3♠. It is good news to West that East has not bid 3♡. Now 3NT is right out of the picture. West continues to bid his shape and East raises the second suit to game. This has to be encouraging for West as East would sign off in 4♠ with a weaker hand, so West presses on to the slam.

Four-card major auction:

West	East
1♠	1NT
3◊	?

Now it is not so clear for East. If West just wanted to find out about three-card spade support, he would not be pleased if East were to bid 3♠. So maybe East should bid 3NT. And if he does bid 3NT it is far from clear for West to bid on. After all East might have 1-5-2-5 distribution. It is all too easy to see the deal played in 6◊ making in one room and 3NT going down in the other.

QUIZ:
DIFFERENCES IN RESPONDING STRATEGY

What would you respond to partner's 1♠ opening with the following hands?

(1)	**(2)**	**(3)**
♠ A 7 3	♠ 9 8 4	♠ K 7 6
♡ K 5	♡ Q 10 5	♡ 8
◊ J 9 4 3	◊ K 9 4 2	◊ A 10 8 7 2
♣ 10 7 6 2	♣ Q J 5	♣ K 9 8 3

What would respond to partner's 1♡ opening with the following hands?

(4)	**(5)**	**(6)**
♠ A 6 5 2	♠ J 9 8 3 2	♠ A K 8 7 3
♡ K 4 3	♡ Q 6 2	♡ 6 5 2
◊ 10 4	◊ A 5	◊ 6 2
♣ J 8 7 2	♣ 8 7 3	♣ 8 7 3

(7)	**(8)**	**(9)**
♠ 8 7	♠ J 8 7 3	♠ K J 10 7 6
♡ K 8 7 2	♡ K 8 7	♡ K 6 5
◊ A J 10 7	◊ A J 8 7 2	◊ A 7 6
♣ 8 7 2	♣ 7	♣ 5 4

You open 1♡ and partner responds 1NT. What do you rebid?

(10)	**(11)**	**(12)**
♠ K J 2	♠ K Q J 5	♠ A 6
♡ A 7 6 5 3	♡ A 7 6 5 3	♡ K J 6 3 2
◊ K Q 6 5	◊ A K 2	◊ A Q J 7
♣ 6	♣ 7	♣ A 6

What would you respond to partner's 1♠ opening with the following hands?

(1)	(2)	(3)
♠ A 7 3	♠ 9 8 4	♠ K 7 6
♡ K 5	♡ Q 10 5	♡ 8
◇ J 9 4 3	◇ K 9 4 2	◇ A 10 8 7 2
♣ 10 7 6 2	♣ Q J 5	♣ K 9 8 3

(1) Raise to 2♠. Even playing four-card majors you should raise partner with three cards to an honour and a ruffing value.

(2) Raise to 2♠. Even with no ruffing value you should raise partner with three-card support.

(3) Raise to 3♠. Here, with good controls and a singleton you can raise directly to the three level when you know partner has a five-card major.

What would respond to partner's 1♡ opening with the following hands?

(4)	(5)	(6)
♠ A 6 5 2	♠ J 9 8 3 2	♠ A K 8 7 3
♡ K 4 3	♡ Q 6 2	♡ 6 5 2
◇ 10 4	◇ A 5	◇ 6 2
♣ J 8 7 2	♣ 8 7 3	♣ 8 7 3

(4) Raise to 2♡. No need to introduce a four-card spade suit when you have a weak hand.

(5) Raise to 2♡. With an honour in hearts and poor spades, the direct raise is better than introducing spades.

(6) Bid 1♠. When spades are the main feature of your hand it is a good idea to get them into the auction. If partner rebids 1NT, you can correct to 2♡. Partner will know you have five spades.

(7)	(8)	(9)
♠ 8 7	♠ J 8 7 3	♠ K J 10 7 6
♡ K 8 7 2	♡ K 8 7	♡ K 6 5
◇ A J 10 7	◇ A J 8 7 2	◇ A 7 6
♣ 8 7 2	♣ 7	♣ 5 4

(7) Raise to 3♡. Use the knowledge of partner's five-card major opposite to help you upgrade your hand when you have four-card support. It pays to overbid a little when you know you have a nine-card fit because the extra trump usually generates an extra trick.

(8) Raise to 3♡. Don't bother with spades or diamonds when you are so suitable for a heart contract.

(9) Bid 1♠. With real invitational values there is no need to hide your spade suit. The more you have the more likely it is that a slam is on if partner has extras, and if that is the case it is best to describe your hand fully.

You open 1♡ and partner responds 1NT. What do you rebid?

(10)	(11)	(12)
♠ K J 2	♠ K Q J 5	♠ A 6
♡ A 7 6 5 3	♡ A 7 6 5 3	♡ K J 6 3 2
◇ K Q 6 5	◇ A K 2	◇ A Q J 7
♣ 6	♣ 7	♣ A 6

(10) Pass. It is most likely that your partner has length/strength in clubs. It could be right to bid 2◇ but you would not be happy if partner were to give you preference to hearts on a doubleton.

(11) Raise to 2NT. You know you don't have an eight-card major-suit fit so invite game in no-trumps and don't help them with the lead.

(12) Raise to 3NT. With such a poor five-card major you know you don't want to play game in it facing a doubleton, so just bid what you think partner can make.

WHAT HAVE WE LEARNED?

A   With a weak responding hand and the choice between raising partner and responding 1NT, always raise partner's major with three-card support.

B   With a weak responding hand and the choice between raising partner's 1♡ opening and responding 1♠, always raise to 2♡ unless the spade suit is a five-carder and most of your values are there.

C   Be prepared to raise partner's five-card major opening to the three level with three-card support when your hand is more suitable for play in the major than no-trumps.

D   Use the knowledge that partner's major is a five-carder to overbid a little when you have four-card support.

E   When you are opener and partner has denied three-card support for your major, don't bid new suits unless there is a real chance you may want to play in them. If there is no eight-card major-suit fit the chances are high that you will want to play in no-trumps.

The 1NT Response

As I explained earlier, when playing the American style it is perfectly acceptable to respond 1NT to an opening of one of a major with up to 10 or 11 points. The only time partner will pass is when he is balanced with 12–14 points, so you will not miss anything.

If you play the French style partner will usually pass the 1NT response when he has 15 or 16 points, so you really need to bid at the two level with a decent 9-count (i.e. one with good spot cards and/or a five-card suit). However, there are also risks attached to bidding at the two level on a 9- or 10-count with a singleton in partner's suit because he might rebid a five-card suit and you will have to guess whether to pass and risk a 5-1 fit or bid 2NT and get too high. However, these problems are similar to the ones Acol players face, so may be what you are used to.

If you play the stronger American style of 1NT response you need to be able to show your extra values when partner does bid on. Obviously if he makes some sort of invitational bid there is no problem – you bid on when you are maximum. However, when he rebids his suit or makes a simple rebid in a new suit you may find it difficult to express your extra values.

How to Show a Maximum 1NT Response

You can do the simple thing, i.e. raise him with a fit and a maximum, bid 2NT with what looks like a bulging 10-count with fitting cards, bid a new suit to show a good suit and a near maximum, but if you are system-minded I will show you a useful toy. You are perhaps familiar with the Lebensohl convention when the opponents come in over your 1NT opening. Well, here a 2NT bid can be used in a similar way:

Consider the sequence:

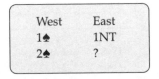

West	East
1♠	1NT
2♠	?

2NT here shows a hand with a long strong suit somewhere, not strong enough for an initial two-level response. Opener bids 3♣ and responder either passes or converts to 3◊ or 3♡, or even 3♠ to show a maximum all-round spade raise.

If instead responder bids 3♣, 3◇ or 3♡ these bids show concentrations of high cards with a spade fit (we are only talking about a doubleton here, of course).

It is more common to use this 2NT bid after opener has bid a new suit:

West	East
1♠	1NT
2♡	2NT
3♣	?

Here a pass shows long clubs and 3◇ shows long diamonds. However, 3♡ shows a maximum, all-round heart raise, and 3♠ a maximum, all-round or heart-based spade raise (the most likely type of hand would be such as ♠Ax ♡KQx ◇Jxxx ♣xxxx, so opener should certainly bid 4♡ with 5-5).

West	East
1♠	1NT
2♡	?

Here 3♣ and 3◇ show concentrations of high cards in a heart or (less likely) spade raise, while 3♡ shows a slightly pre-emptive heart raise.

Let's look at a few examples:

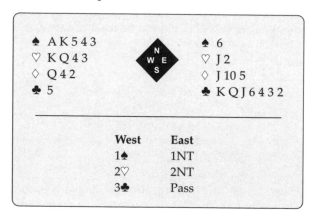

♠ A K 5 4 3   ♠ 6
♡ K Q 4 3   ♡ J 2
◇ Q 4 2   ◇ J 10 5
♣ 5   ♣ K Q J 6 4 3 2

West	East
1♠	1NT
2♡	2NT
3♣	Pass

All East wants to do when West opens 1♠ and rebids 2♡ is to sign off in 3♣. He does this by bidding 2NT and passing his partner's 3♣ bid.

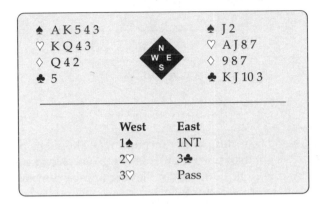

	♠ A K 5 4 3			♠ J 2
	♡ K Q 4 3			♡ A J 8 7
	◇ Q 4 2			◇ 9 8 7
	♣ 5			♣ K J 10 3

West	East
1♠	1NT
2♡	3♣
3♡	Pass

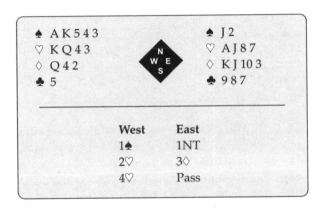

	♠ A K 5 4 3			♠ J 2
	♡ K Q 4 3			♡ A J 8 7
	◇ Q 4 2			◇ K J 10 3
	♣ 5			♣ 9 8 7

West	East
1♠	1NT
2♡	3◇
4♡	Pass

Knowing where responder's high cards are can allow opener to evaluate his hand. As soon as opener rebids a new suit, it is likely that his distribution is 5-4-3-1. If responder has kings and queens they will clearly be much more useful if they are in opener's three-card suit than facing his singleton.

Should Opener Pass 1NT or Rebid a Second Suit?

Suppose opener holds a hand such as:

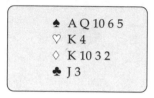

♠ A Q 10 6 5
♡ K 4
◇ K 10 3 2
♣ J 3

He opens 1♠ and hears his partner respond 1NT. Should he pass or bid 2◇? When we learn the game we are told to bid our second suit but this is not always the right thing to do. Playing four-card majors partner could have either of the hands below:

	(1)		(2)
♠	7	♠	K 9 3
♡	Q J 10 7 2	♡	7 6 2
◇	Q 9 4	◇	A J 9 4
♣	K 10 9 2	♣	8 5 2

Facing Hand (1) 1NT is by far the best spot, while facing Hand (2) 4♠ is about as good a contract as 1NT. But, of course, playing five-card majors you know that partner cannot have Hand (2) or any other hand with three-card support for your major. This knowledge makes it much less likely to be right to bid over 1NT.

Playing five-card majors, think twice about introducing a new four-card minor after partner responds 1NT. If you open 1♡ and have a singleton spade, then you must rebid your minor because partner, with at least eight minor-suit cards, is likely to have a fit with you; the opponents may compete in spades in a moment and you need to know how good a minor-suit fit you have. But otherwise give consideration to passing 1NT as partner will usually have values and length in your short suits. This can work particularly well when you are minimum with 5-4-2-2 or 5-4-3-1 with a singleton honour or when your long suits are weak. Partner may have 10 or 11 points for his 1NT response and if you rebid your second suit he may bid on with some enthusiasm. If you would be happy for him to do this – say you have 14 or 15 points – then rebid your second suit, otherwise consider passing.

QUIZ: THE 1NT RESPONSE

What do you respond to your partner's 1♠ opening with these hands?

	(1)	**(2)**	**(3)**
♠	5	10 6	J 6 5
♡	K Q J 10 5 4	K J 6 5	K 4 3
◇	K 6 5	K Q 5 4	A 6 3 2
♣	8 7 2	Q 7 6	8 7 6

Your partner responds 1NT to your 1♠ opening. What do you rebid?

	(4)	**(5)**	**(6)**
♠	A J 7 5 3	K Q 10 6 5	A Q 10 6 5
♡	K	A 6	K J 6 5
◇	K J 5 4	A Q 4 3	K 2
♣	J 5 4	7 6	6 5

Partner opens 1♠, you respond 1NT and he rebids 2◇. What do you bid?

	(7)	**(8)**	**(9)**
♠	7	7	7
♡	K Q 10 9 4 3	A Q J 10 6 5	K Q 5 4
◇	6 5	6 5 2	A 10 7 6 2
♣	8 7 3 2	Q 6 5	8 7 6

	(10)	**(11)**	**(12)**
♠	K 5	K Q	7
♡	7 6 3 2	A 8 7 3	8 7
◇	K 10 6 5	Q 7 6	K Q 7 4 3
♣	7 6 3	8 7 3 2	K J 6 5 2

What do you respond to your partner's 1♠ opening with these hands?

(1)	(2)	(3)
♠ 5	♠ 10 6	♠ J 6 5
♡ K Q J 10 5 4	♡ K J 6 5	♡ K 4 3
◇ K 6 5	◇ K Q 5 4	◇ A 6 3 2
♣ 8 7 2	♣ Q 7 6	♣ 8 7 6

(1) Playing Acol, 2♡ would be clear, but it isn't really good enough for a two-level response playing these methods. Respond 1NT.

(2) Respond 1NT. It would be too good playing Acol, but it really isn't a very good 11 and you know that partner doesn't have 15–17 and a balanced hand.

(3) Raise to 2♠. Just to make sure you haven't forgotten what you learnt earlier!

Your partner responds 1NT to your 1♠ opening. What do you rebid?

(4)	(5)	(6)
♠ A J 7 5 3	♠ K Q 10 6 5	♠ A Q 10 6 5
♡ K	♡ A 6	♡ K J 6 5
◇ K J 5 4	◇ A Q 4 3	◇ K 2
♣ J 5 4	♣ 7 6	♣ 6 5

(4) Pass. Partner probably has length/strength in hearts, and in any event you do not want to give him the chance to bid on.

(5) Here you are stronger and would be delighted to hear him make some forward-going move, so rebid 2◇.

(6) Rebid 2♡. If your second suit were a minor you would pass, but you don't want to risk missing 4♡ if partner has length there and a maximum, so rebid your second suit.

Partner opens 1♠, you respond 1NT and he rebids 2◇. What do you bid?

(7)	(8)	(9)
♠ 7	♠ 7	♠ 7
♡ K Q 10 9 4 3	♡ A Q J 10 6 5	♡ K Q 5 4
◇ 6 5	◇ 6 5 2	◇ A 10 7 6 2
♣ 8 7 3 2	♣ Q 6 5	♣ 8 7 6

(7) Bid 2♡. A sign-off. Just as you would do playing any other method.

(8) Here you want to show your own heart suit but with a good hand. Start with 2NT and bid 3♡ over partner's 3♣ to show your own good suit in a maximum 1NT.

(9) A rebid of 3♡ on this hand is slightly pushy but describes the hand well: heart values with a good diamond fit. The trouble is that if partner is unsuitable 4◇ may go down. A more conservative approach would be to bid 2NT and convert 3♣ to 3◇, simply showing a good diamond raise – at least partner will know you don't have concentrated values in clubs.

(10)	(11)	(12)
♠ K 5	♠ K Q	♠ 7
♡ 7 6 3 2	♡ A 8 7 3	♡ 8 7
◇ K 10 6 5	◇ Q 7 6	◇ K Q 7 4 3
♣ 7 6 3	♣ 8 7 3 2	♣ K J 6 5 2

(10) You could pass, but with two useful kings you would be happy if partner were to continue. I would give simple preference to 2♠, which at Pairs scoring might be the winner anyway.

(11) Bid 2NT and follow up with 3♠ to show a partial spade fit and good all-round values.

(12) Bid 3♣, showing a good hand for diamonds with club values.

WHAT HAVE WE LEARNED?

A   Playing the American style of strong no-trump and five-card majors, the initial 1NT response denies three-card support for opener's major but can be up to a poor 11 points.

B   Opener should pass a 1NT response rather than rebid a second suit on a 5-4 hand unless either (1) his suits are good, or (2) he would welcome his partner bidding on. However, if his second suit is hearts he should rebid it unless he has a truly dreadful hand.

C   If opener does rebid a new suit and responder is maximum he should try to make an encouraging noise. All direct bids at the three level in a new suit show a fit for one of opener's suits, while a 2NT rebid is either a prelude to signing off in responder's long suit, or else shows all-round values and support for opener's second (occasionally first) suit.

D   When deciding whether to pass opener's second suit or give preference to his first suit be swayed by whether or not you would like to hear him bid on; with a weak hand pass, but with extra values give preference.

The 2NT Rebid and Two-over-one Response

As I have said earlier, the method is different depending on whether you go for the American or French styles. The French style is very similar to normal Acol and I will not go into it any further here.

The Americans play that a two-over-one response shows 11 or more points, though it can be a little lighter if a long strong suit is held. It promises another bid, so the sequence 1♠ – 2♣ – 2♠ is forcing, which means that 1♠ – 2♣ – 3♠ shows a self-supporting, at-most-one-loser suit. Because the response is necessarily stronger than in Acol it makes sense to play some other sequences as forcing, e.g. 1♠ – 2♣ – 2♡ – 3♡.

The 2NT rebid shows a minimum 12–14 opener and will be passed only if responder has a rock bottom 11-count. In truth, 2NT is not the right contract very often. Rather than regularly playing in 2NT, it is surely better to stay low in 1NT when the hands do not seem to fit well and overbid to 3NT whenever it has a chance of making; go for the plus score (by staying in 1NT) or the game bonus (by bidding 3NT), but don't make a habit of languishing in the middle.

Here are some examples of how this American system works:

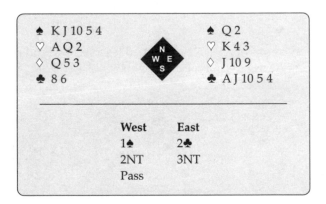

♠ KJ 10 5 4		♠ Q 2
♡ A Q 2		♡ K 4 3
◇ Q 5 3		◇ J 10 9
♣ 8 6		♣ A J 10 5 4

West	East
1♠	2♣
2NT	3NT
Pass	

Although East has only 11 points, A-J-10 is a good combination and the queen of spades must be a good card. On a diamond lead the suit needs to break 4-3, and a club lead through dummy's suit could pose a problem if both honours are wrong, but all-in-all 3NT has to be favourite to make.

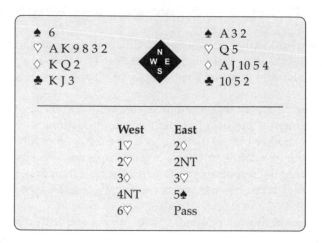

	♠ 6		♠ A 3 2
	♡ A K 9 8 3 2		♡ Q 5
	◇ K Q 2		◇ A J 10 5 4
	♣ K J 3		♣ 10 5 2

West	East
1♡	2◇
2♡	2NT
3◇	3♡
4NT	5♠
6♡	Pass

Although the outcome would probably be the same playing Acol, this has been a comfortable auction for the American style. West has been able to keep the bidding low with his good hand and not-so-brilliant suit. He has heard his partner make a limited, non-forcing rebid. As soon as West bids over this the partnership is in a game force (would this sequence be forcing in Acol?), so West can show his diamond support in comfort. When East shows his doubleton honour in hearts West uses Roman Key Card Blackwood (RKCB) to arrive at the good slam.

The auction would not be so easy in Acol because it would be hard for East to agree hearts unequivocally and show his two aces.

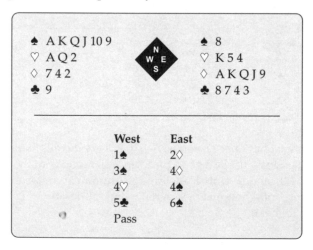

	♠ A K Q J 10 9		♠ 8
	♡ A Q 2		♡ K 5 4
	◇ 7 4 2		◇ A K Q J 9
	♣ 9		♣ 8 7 4 3

West	East
1♠	2◇
3♠	4◇
4♡	4♠
5♣	6♠
Pass	

Here, because West's jump rebid shows at worst a one-loser suit, East's four diamond bid agrees spades. West first cue-bids his ace and then goes on to show his second-round club control. That is enough for East, with all his diamond tricks, to bid the slam.

Playing Acol it is not so clear that East's four diamonds agrees spades, or even if it does, that it is what East wants to do. Without knowledge of the solidity of the spade suit opposite it is much harder to bid the slam.

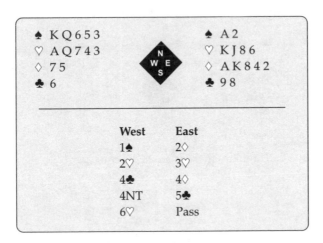

	♠ KQ653		♠ A2
	♡ AQ743	N	♡ KJ86
	◊ 75	W E	◊ AK842
	♣ 6	S	♣ 98

West	East
1♠	2◊
2♡	3♡
4♣	4◊
4NT	5♣
6♡	Pass

Here the ability to make a forcing raise to 3♡ makes the auction easy for East-West. There are several alternative routes, but all reach the small slam easily enough.

The Acol auction is much more difficult: over 2♡ East has to bid 3♣, fourth-suit forcing. West rebids 3♡. East still does not have an unequivocal, forcing way to agree hearts. He has to guess: either to settle for 4♡, or else perhaps to give a false preference to 3♠ in the hope that West will cue-bid 4♣, whereupon East can leap to 6♡ and hope West gets the message.

Raising Partner

Game Tries after a Simple Raise

In the section on *Differences in Responding Strategy* we agreed that we would make a simple raise of partner's suit on any hand in the right range with three-card support. One of the great strengths of five-card majors is that because the fit is found so quickly, the rest of the auction on some deals can be devoted to deciding whether or not to play in that fit. Playing four-card majors, too much time can be wasted simply discovering if there is an eight-card fit at all. Look at the following two hands:

Playing five-card majors there is an easy sequence:

Playing four-card majors there are some problems. First, does West rebid 2NT when he has a five-card spade suit? If he does bid 2NT what does East bid? He has the values to accept the game try but does not know whether to choose 4♠, which would be perfect facing the West hand above, or 3NT which would clearly be right facing, for example:

```
♠ K 8 7 3
♡ K 10
◇ K Q J 8
♣ K Q 2
```

There is no reason why West should not hold this hand and 4♠ is a rather silly contract. It is possible, however, that 4♠ on a 4-3 fit is the right contract, but East-West have no way of investigating this. Most partnerships would play that a 3♣ bid from East over 2NT is a wish to play there, and if that is the case East has no option but to guess.

Perhaps you will say that, playing four-card majors, West should not rebid 2NT with a five-card suit. In that case, how should the following pair of hands be bid?

Here 3NT is clearly the contract of choice, and would be reached easily via 1♠ – 2♠ – 2NT – 3NT. But now West cannot rebid 2NT, so chooses, say, 3◊. Now it looks natural for East to plump for 4♠ with his useful queen doubleton in diamonds. He does not know that West has a balanced hand.

These hands are much easier to judge when the 5-3 fit is established immediately and known to both players.

The Importance of Distributional Features

No doubt it would work reasonably well to make jump raises in the same way as we are used to in a four-card major style, i.e. play normal limit raises, with raises to both levels containing either three- or four-card support. But perhaps we can aim higher…

When bridge was first played the power of distribution was not understood in quite the same way as it is today.

There are 40 points in the pack and thirteen tricks. Therefore, roughly speaking, each 3 points makes one trick. So, to make 3NT, according to this theory, you would need 27 points. A little generous, perhaps, but not so far off beam.

Now suppose you hold a thirteen-card suit and your partner has a Yarborough. You will make thirteen tricks with only 10 points. Hands with five-, six- and seven-card suits come somewhere in between. But the general principle is that long suits can be just as valuable, if not more so, than high-card points.

Now let's consider the straightforward play of a hand with a trump fit. Suppose you have a solid trump fit. What you would like to do is draw trumps but then maybe have some trumps left over.

- If you have a 4-4 fit, most of the time you will draw three rounds of trumps and then have a trump left in each hand. In total you will make five trump tricks.
- If you have a 5-3 fit you will draw three rounds of trumps and then have two left in one hand but none in the other. Again you will make five tricks.
- If you have a 5-4 fit, most of the time you will have to draw three rounds of trumps but then will have one left in one hand and two left in the other, giving you a total of six tricks. However, about 40% of the time you will need to draw only two rounds for the opponents' trumps will break 2-2. In those cases you will make seven tricks.
- If you have a 5-5 fit you would expect to draw trumps in two rounds and then have three left in each hand, making a total of eight tricks altogether.

So when you progress beyond an eight-card fit, you can make about one and a half tricks extra for each extra trump you have, provided, of course, that you have something to ruff.

Let's carry on with this arithmetical exercise. If you need, say, a combined 25 points to make game in a major, that is about 2.5 points per trick. So you would need 25 − (1.5 x 2.5), i.e. 25 − 3.75 = 21.25 points to make game with a nine-card fit, or 17.5 points to make game with a ten-card fit.

Obviously that is rather simplistic and there are plenty of other factors to take into account; in particular you need to have things you want to ruff. That is why singletons and voids are important. But you get the general idea. THE DEGREE OF FIT IS ENORMOUSLY IMPORTANT.

The Law of Total Tricks

Another piece of arithmetic tells us that if we have a good fit then so do our opponents. Suppose, for example, that we have a nine-card fit; i.e. out of our 26 cards, nine are, say, spades. Therefore we have 17 non-spades. The most evenly distributed those 17 cards can be is 6-6-5. So it is a mathematical certainty that our opponents have an eight-card fit. And much more often they will also hold a nine-card fit. If we have an eight-card fit then the only time they will not have an eight-card fit is when they have three seven-card fits.

So, generally speaking, the greater the fit, the more tricks we can make but also the more tricks the opponents can make too. This is well expressed in the Law of Total Tricks and I quote *The Official Encyclopedia of Bridge*:

> **Law of Total Tricks** The theory that on any given bridge deal the total number of trumps will approximate the total number of tricks available on that deal. The total number of trumps is obtained by adding North-South's longest trump fit to East-West's longest trump fit. The total number of tricks is the sum of the number of tricks North-South would take playing in their best fit and the number of tricks East-West would take playing in their best fit.

While we five-card-majorites are well placed to find the 5-3 fits, what do we do when we have four-card support? If a three-card major-suit raise shows about 6–10 points, and we need nearly 4 points fewer to make game with four-card support, then should we be making a jump raise when we have four-card support and only 2–6 points?

No, not really. It is true that that extra trump is very important but probably only worth a couple of points on most hands. If it can be established that opener has length in a suit in which we have a singleton then the hands will fit well and fewer points will be needed for game, but generally the extra trump is worth only 2 points. But that still means that a simple raise should be made with about 4 to 8 points if we are talking about equivalent value.

Perhaps the four-card-majorites would argue that they are better placed here because with them the raise would generally show four-card support, making it easier for opener to press on when he has five. The problem is that they don't really know that the raise has been made with four trumps because three-card support with a potential ruffing value is sufficient for most pairs.

Also, it is one thing to say that three-card support with 6–10 points is equivalent to four-card support with 4–8 points in an uncontested auction when we are talking about freely bidding our games, but what if the opponents intervene? This is something we will deal with in more detail in the next section, but it is easy to see that if we are to apply the Law of Total Tricks we need to know how many trumps we have between us. It is generally right to bid on to the three level when we have nine trumps but if we do that consistently when we have only eight we could find both contracts going down. In this situation a 6-count with four-card support is not the same as an 8-count with three-card support.

Because we know of the five-card major opposite, it is fairly safe to try to get in the way of the opponents' constructive auction by pushing the bidding to the three level more or less whenever we have four-card support. It is much riskier for Acolites to do this. To push the bidding to the three level on a few points and four-card support is not sound when partner is quite likely to have a strong no-trump with only a four-card major. In fact, one of the advantages that the Acol system has is that they can play in a 4-4 fit in a part-score when they have, say a balanced 15–16 count facing 6–8. If they force all these hands to the three level then they have lost that edge.

Bergen Raises

Because the American style is to play strong two-over one responses it is possible to have controlled auctions when responder is strong as we saw on pages 33–5. The traditional jump-shift response at the three level is not needed nearly as much as it is in Acol. So the system played by most American tournament players is to keep strong jump-shifts at the two level but to use a jump to three of a minor to show a raise of partner's suit.

The original method was devised by Marty Bergen: in response to an opening one of a major, a 3♣ response showed 7–10 points with four trumps, a 3◊ response showed more, i.e. a limit raise, and a direct jump raise showed 0–7 points with four or more trumps.

This method ties in neatly with a forcing 1NT response which I am not going to advocate here but will look at later in Part III. However, if you are not keen on a forcing 1NT response (and I am not), then I have found the following variation on the Bergen raise to be useful:

- A 3♣ response shows 10–12 points with *three*-card support
- A 3◇ response shows about 8–11 with *four*-card support
- A jump raise shows 0–7 as recommended by Bergen (in my view partner should expect four trumps, one useful outside high card and a doubleton)

This makes it easy to distinguish between three-card and four-card support and helps partner to judge slam expectations and whether or not to bid on if the opponents intervene.

Here are some example hands:

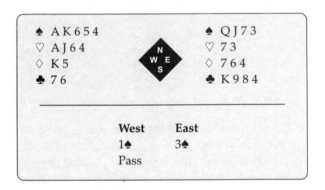

West's 5-4-2-2 distribution is not very exciting and even 3♠ may be too high facing partner's near-maximum pre-emptive raise.

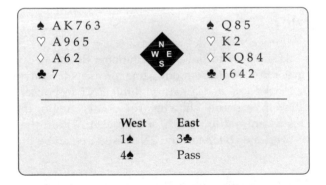

Despite East's well-fitting collection, slam is not really good here although twelve tricks may often be made. To start with, a 3-2 trump fit is needed, which happens only 68% of the time. Then declarer needs either (1) to ruff two hearts in the dummy which will only happen without promoting a spade loser for declarer when North has three hearts and three spades, or (2) ruff one heart in the dummy and hope diamonds are 3-3 or a squeeze develops.

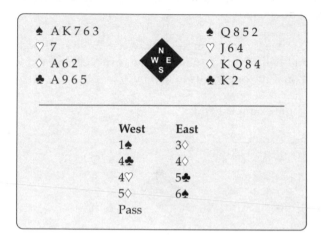

♠ AK763
♡ 7
♢ A62
♣ A965

♠ Q852
♡ J64
♢ KQ84
♣ K2

West	East
1♠	3♢
4♣	4♢
4♡	5♣
5♢	6♠
Pass	

When East has a fourth trump the slam becomes good. West's 4♣ is natural and East shows his diamond feature along with his useful club holding. That suits the West hand well – if East is prepared to co-operate on an aceless hand he must surely have good minor-suit holdings. West shows his heart control, East confirms that he has a club honour, West shows his diamond control and East jumps to slam.

Jacoby 2NT

So we now know how to bid our invitational fit hands opposite our five-card major but what about our game forces? Not many traditional Acol players have retained a natural, limit, 2NT response, but many prefer to play it as Baron, showing 16+ points. Again, these strong balanced hands are not too much of a problem within the American strong two-over-one style, and the 2NT response can be put to better use.

Oswald Jacoby was the first to develop the idea of using a 2NT response as showing a game force with four-card support for opener. The idea was that it showed a balanced hand with at least four-card support and game values. Distributional hands either use immediate splinter bids or some other device.

The original schedule of further bidding was for a simple rebid in a new suit to show a singleton in that suit and for a four-level bid in a new suit to show a 5-5 hand. More balanced hands were shown via a jump to game (about 12–13), a 3NT rebid (about 14–15) or a simple rebid in the suit opened (about 16–17). This is the method played by many Americans today, though there are plenty of variations made by individual partnerships.

Let's look at some examples:

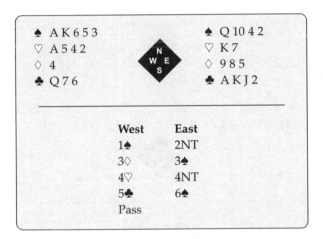

	♠ A K 6 5 3			♠ Q 10 4 2
	♡ A 5 4 2			♡ K 7
	◇ 4			◇ 9 8 5
	♣ Q 7 6			♣ A K J 2

West	East
1♠	2NT
3◇	3♠
4♡	4NT
5♣	6♠
Pass	

Once West shows a singleton diamond, East's hand looks very suitable. He shows he is still interested by bidding 3♠ and West cue-bids his ace of hearts. East now knows that slam is unlikely to be worse than on a finesse so checks up on aces via RKCB and bids the slam when he finds he is facing three.

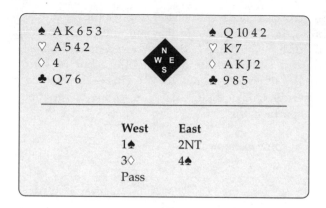

	♠ AK653		♠ Q1042
	♡ A542		♡ K7
	◇ 4		◇ AKJ2
	♣ Q76		♣ 985

West	East
1♠	2NT
3◇	4♠
Pass	

Now the singleton is bad news and East shows this by signing off in game.

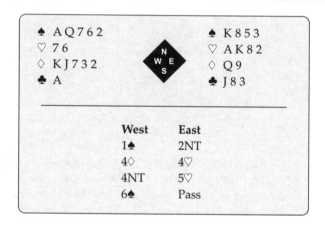

	♠ AQ762		♠ K853
	♡ 76		♡ AK82
	◇ KJ732		◇ Q9
	♣ A		♣ J83

West	East
1♠	2NT
4◇	4♡
4NT	5♡
6♠	Pass

East's 4♡ cue-bid does not just show a heart control, it also implies a helpful diamond holding, or else significant extra values. The cue-bid is quite rightly enough to persuade West to use RKCB and bid the slam facing two 'aces'.

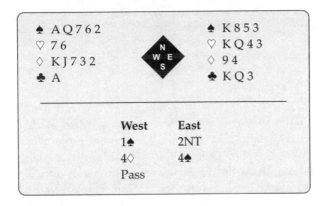

	♠ A Q 7 6 2		♠ K 8 5 3
	♡ 7 6		♡ K Q 4 3
	◇ K J 7 3 2		◇ 9 4
	♣ A		♣ K Q 3

West	East
1♠	2NT
4◇	4♠
Pass	

Here, with two small diamonds, East is not tempted to cue-bid his second-round heart control. As well as having no aces, East has too many of his values outside West's long suits. If a heart control is all that West needs he can bid again.

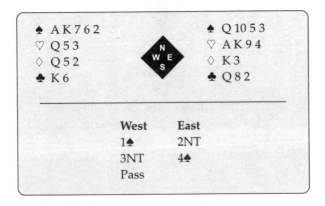

	♠ A K 7 6 2		♠ Q 10 5 3
	♡ Q 5 3		♡ A K 9 4
	◇ Q 5 2		◇ K 3
	♣ K 6		♣ Q 8 2

West	East
1♠	2NT
3NT	4♠
Pass	

With two balanced hands facing each other it is difficult to tell whether or not they fit well. These are the hands where relay systems come into their own. All natural bidders can do is bid on general values, upgrading good controls. Here East knows that the combined values are in the 28–29 point area and that slam could be on if they fit well but is probably odds against. Here even if either side were to view their hand more rosily, RKCB would prevent a disaster.

Note that if West had the ace of clubs instead of the king, and rebid 3♣, then slam would be fair, usually depending on the hearts to come in or possibly a squeeze. On a club lead declarer would have to decide on the likelihood of North underleading the king of clubs: if he has it then playing the queen from dummy gives the slam immediately, but it destroys the club menace if it is wrong.

The 3NT Response

The most efficient way to play a 3NT response allied to these methods is as a natural balanced hand in the 13–15 point range with three-card support for the major. One of the advantages of playing five-card majors is that, once the fit is found, both hands can consider the desirability of playing in no-trumps instead. Playing four-card majors, often all that can be managed is establishing that an eight-card fit exists at all.

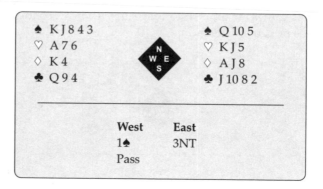

	West	East
	1♠	3NT
	Pass	

With two balanced hands, there is no need to look beyond 3NT for the final contract.

Splinter Bids

The final tool in the raising-partner armoury is the splinter bid which is in widespread use whatever the basic method used. Traditional US methods are to play these as unlimited, but in my view that is unwieldy. Opener needs to know what sort of values he can expect in order to know whether to be enthusiastic with a suitable minimum opening. I think splinter bids are best played as limited to about 10–12 points. It does not take much for slam to be on with that range facing a suitable opening. Stronger hands with a shortage should start with a Jacoby 2NT.

QUIZ: RAISING PARTNER

Partner opens 1♠. What do you respond holding?

(1)
♠ Q J 5
♡ Q 10 5 4
◊ K 7 6
♣ Q 6 4

(2)
♠ K 7 6
♡ 5
◊ A Q 9 8 2
♣ 10 9 4 3

(3)
♠ J 10 5 4
♡ 7
◊ K 10 4 3
♣ 9 8 4 3

(4)
♠ K Q 6 5
♡ A 10 7 6
◊ 8 7
♣ J 10 7

(5)
♠ A Q 7 6
♡ 8
◊ K J 6
♣ J 10 6 5 2

(6)
♠ J 10 8 7 3
♡ 6
◊ K 10 6 5 2
♣ 6 5

(7)
♠ J 10 4
♡ K J 6
◊ A Q 6 2
♣ K 9 4

(8)
♠ A 10 7 6
♡ K 10
◊ A 9 8 7 2
♣ 7 6

(9)
♠ A Q 2
♡ 8 7
◊ K J 10 7
♣ J 10 6 5

(10)
♠ 8 7 6 3
♡ K J 7
◊ J 10 4
♣ K 4 3

(11)
♠ A K 6 5
♡ A K J 10 5 4
◊ 7
♣ 9 2

(12)
♠ 10 9 5 4
♡ A J 10 7 6
◊ 7
♣ 10 9 5

(13)
♠ K J 6 5
♡ 6
◊ A Q 7 6 2
♣ A 10 6

(14)
♠ A Q 2
♡ 5 4
◊ A Q J 4 3
♣ 8 7 3

(15)
♠ K J 7
♡ 6
◊ A K 8 7 3
♣ A 7 6 2

Partner opens 1♠. What do you respond holding?

(1)	(2)	(3)
♠ Q J 5	♠ K 7 6	♠ J 10 5 4
♡ Q 10 5 4	♡ 5	♡ 7
◊ K 7 6	◊ A Q 9 8 2	◊ K 10 4 3
♣ Q 6 4	♣ 10 9 4 3	♣ 9 8 4 3

(1) Raise to 2♠. This hand is not worth a three-level bid. It is a dreadful 10-count. It is unlikely you will miss anything if you make a simple raise.

(2) Bid 3♣. This may be only a 9-count but it is a hugely better hand than the previous one. Show your support immediately with a three-card limit raise.

(3) Bid 3♠. A pre-emptive raise is what you've got. If the next hand intervenes, partner should be able to judge whether or not to bid on.

(4)	(5)	(6)
♠ K Q 6 5	♠ A Q 7 6	♠ J 10 8 7 3
♡ A 10 7 6	♡ 8	♡ 6
◊ 8 7	◊ K J 6	◊ K 10 6 5 2
♣ J 10 7	♣ J 10 6 5 2	♣ 6 5

(4) Bid 3◊. A normal limit raise.

(5) Bid 4♡. This hand is perfect for a 4♡ splinter. You need partner's hand to fit well for a slam to be on.

(6) Bid 4♠. Someone once said that if you know you have a ten-card spade fit you should always bid 4♠. If it doesn't make it will be a good sacrifice against something. Partner will not play you to have much.

(7)	(8)	(9)
♠ J 10 4	♠ A 10 7 6	♠ A Q 2
♡ K J 6	♡ K 10	♡ 8 7
♢ A Q 6 2	♢ A 9 8 7 2	♢ K J 10 7
♣ K 9 4	♣ 7 6	♣ J 10 6 5

(7) Bid 3NT. If partner also has a balanced hand the nine-trick game should be safer.

(8) Bid 2NT. This may be only an 11-count but it is too good for a limit raise. Show game-forcing values and leave the rest to partner.

(9) Bid 3♣. This is a normal three-card limit raise: a useful-looking 10–12-count with a ruffing value.

(10)	(11)	(12)
♠ 8 7 6 3	♠ A K 6 5	♠ 10 9 5 4
♡ K J 7	♡ A K J 10 5 4	♡ A J 10 7 6
♢ J 10 4	♢ 7	♢ 7
♣ K 4 3	♣ 9 2	♣ 10 9 5

(10) Bid 2♠. I know you have four-card support, but 4-3-3-3 distribution is horrible and your spades are poor.

(11) Bid 3♡. An Acol-style force. If partner rebids 3♠ you can cue-bid 4♢ to show your control and your spade support. If partner then signs off, a raise to 5♠ describes your hand well: if you had a club control you would have bid it; if you had a similar hand but with first-round diamond control you would have repeated your diamond cue-bid.

(12) This is tricky and anything could be right. It's too good I think for a pre-emptive raise, so it's a choice between 3♢ and 4♠. I'd bid 4♠ non-vulnerable, for its pre-emptive effect, but settle for 3♢ vulnerable and leave it to partner.

(13)	(14)	(15)
♠ K J 6 5	♠ A Q 2	♠ K J 7
♡ 6	♡ 5 4	♡ 6
◊ A Q 7 6 2	◊ A Q J 4 3	◊ A K 8 7 3
♣ A 10 6	♣ 8 7 3	♣ A 7 6 2

(13) Bid 2NT. This hand is too good for a 4♡ splinter because if partner signs off you won't know whether or not to bid on.

(14) Bid 2◊. When you have the values for game you can afford to take it slowly. It would be a mistake to bid 3NT with a ruffing value and two suits unguarded – you are too suitable for a spade contract.

(15) Bid 2◊. When you have a strong hand there is no reason not to bid it naturally. If partner rebids 2♠ you can splinter with 4♡ on the next round, showing just three-card support.

Choose your next bid on the following hands after the auctions given below:

(1)
♠ A Q 6 5 3
♡ K 6 5
◊ K 2
♣ A J 8

1♠   3♣
?

(2)
♠ A 7 6
♡ 8
◊ K J 8 7 3
♣ 8 7 4 3

1♠   2♠
2NT ?

(3)
♠ K 9 8 4
♡ Q 6
◊ A J 10 8
♣ 7 6 2

1♠   3◊
3♡   ?

(4)
♠ 8
♡ K J 10 6 5 2
◊ Q 4
♣ A 6 5 3

1♡   3◊
?

(5)
♠ K J 10 4
♡ Q 6
◊ A 8 7 6
♣ A 5 4

1♠   2NT
4♡   ?

(6)
♠ A Q 5 4
♡ K 10 6 5 2
◊ 8
♣ 9 8 7

1♡   ?

(7)
♠ K 7 6
♡ A 10 7 2
◊ K Q J 7 3
♣ 6

1♠   2◊
2♠   ?

(8)
♠ 7
♡ A Q 7 6 3
◊ K 10 6 5 2
♣ Q 5

1♡   3NT
?

(9)
♠ A J 6 5 2
♡ 7
◊ K Q 6 5
♣ Q 10 3

1♠   2NT
3♡   3♠
?

Choose your next bid on the following hands after the auctions given:

	(1)		(2)		(3)
♠	A Q 6 5 3	♠	A 7 6	♠	K 9 8 4
♡	K 6 5	♡	8	♡	Q 6
◇	K 2	◇	K J 8 7 3	◇	A J 10 8
♣	A J 8	♣	8 7 4 3	♣	7 6 2

1♠	3♣	1♠	2♠	1♠	3◇
?		2NT	?	3♡	?

(1) Bid 3NT, showing a balanced hand, and leave the rest to partner. If he has a singleton, or even a small doubleton, he will go back to 4♠.

(2) Bid 4♠. Partner has a strong balanced hand but your hand is much better for suit play. Bid game in your known 5-3 fit.

(3) Bid 4◇. Partner's 3♡ might be a further game try or maybe he is interested in a slam. In either case you are happy to co-operate because your queen of hearts should be pulling its weight, while if he is interested in a slam he will want to know about your diamond control.

	(4)		(5)		(6)
♠	8	♠	K J 10 4	♠	A Q 5 4
♡	K J 10 6 5 2	♡	Q 6	♡	K 10 6 5 2
◇	Q 4	◇	A 8 7 6	◇	8
♣	A 6 5 3	♣	A 5 4	♣	9 8 7

1♡	3◇	1♠	2NT	1♡	?
?		4♡	?		

(4) Bid 4♡. When you have a ten-card major-suit fit you don't need much of an excuse to bid game.

(5) 4NT. Partner is 5-5 in the majors and your hand is extremely suitable. Start by checking up on aces. If he bids 5♠ to show two aces and the queen of trumps, continue with 5NT to ask about kings. This will tell him that you hold all the aces between you and should encourage him to bid the grand slam if he also has the king of hearts.

(6) Bid 4◊. Although you have only 9 high-card points, a 5-5 major-suit fit is very powerful, so you are just worth a splinter bid.

(7)	(8)	(9)
♠ K 7 6	♠ 7	♠ A J 6 5 2
♡ A 10 7 2	♡ A Q 7 6 3	♡ 7
◊ K Q J 7 3	◊ K 10 6 5 2	◊ K Q 6 5
♣ 6	♣ Q 5	♣ Q 10 3
1♠ 2◊	1♡ 3NT	1♠ 2NT
2♠ ?	?	3♡ 3♠
		?

(7) Bid 4♣. A splinter bid but with only three spades (or you would have bid it on the first round).

(8) Bid 4♡. 4◊ here would be a slam try and you are not worth that. Partner has promised three hearts, though, so you should bid the game in your major suit.

(9) Bid 4♠. You have already shown your singleton. Now partner wants to know if you have extra values. With your minimum opening bid you should settle for 4♠.

WHAT HAVE WE LEARNED?

A   Develop bidding judgement. Distribution is at least as important as high-card points, even when valuing balanced hands. 4-4-3-2 is much better than 4-3-3-3, whether you are considering a suit contract or no-trumps. Other things to look for are having your high-card points together in one or two suits rather than spread about the hand, and also give some value to tens and nines which are generally more useful than twos and threes.

B   If you have a game-force with three-card support for partner, bid it naturally.

C   Bid aggressively when you have four- or five-card support for the five-card major.

Bidding after Intervention

When the opponents join in, it is even more important to exchange information about the degree of fit. Here are some general rules:

- Simple raises show three-card support.
- Jump raises show four cards or more in support but little in the way of high-card values.
- A cue-bid of the opponent's suit shows at least the values for a limit raise usually with four-card support, but occasionally three-card support and a suit-oriented hand.
- A jump in a new suit shows length/strength in that suit along with a fit for opener. Some people like to play this fit-jump as showing four-card support but I am happy that it delivers three-card support at the three level (and is forcing only to three of the suit opened) and four-card support at the four level.

The common problem hand is one too good for a simple raise but with only three-card support and no strong side-suit suitable for a fit-jump. How you deal with this problem depends on your general attitude; it is possible to use, for example, a 2NT response to deal with this hand-type. The alternative is just to do the best with the tools already available. If I am balanced the opponents are unlikely to do anything too wild and I am happy to start with a negative double. On the other hand, if I am more suit-oriented I am happy to lie and call it a four-card raise.

The Opponents Double

Generally, bidding is as you would expect.

- Simple bids in new suits are forcing for one round.
- Raises are normal with 2NT showing a limit raise or better. With three-card support and 10+ points you can redouble first and show your support later.
- Jumps in new suits should be fit-jumps. Fit-jumps are a good modern invention, but do remember that when you make any bid other than raising partner you give the opponents more room. Suppose you have a 3-1-5-4 distribution: if partner opens 1♠ and the next hand doubles if you make a fit-jump of 3◊ you allow the next hand an easy 3♡ bid. Be sure that you think making the descriptive bid is worth the price.

Here are some examples:

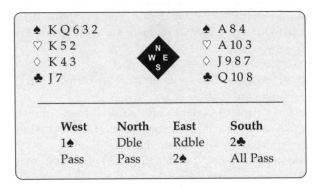

West	North	East	South
1♠	Dble	Rdble	2♣
Pass	Pass	2♠	All Pass

Without North's helpful take-out double East would surely have responded 3♣ and the partnership would have had to play unsafely at the three level, but here East can redouble and then settle for a simple 2♠. There would be no reason for East-West to bid on even if North-South pressed on to 3♣.

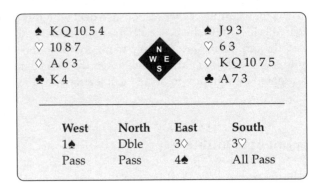

West	North	East	South
1♠	Dble	3◇	3♡
Pass	Pass	4♠	All Pass

Here, with such suitability for spade play and a good diamond suit, East risks allowing South into the auction. With a minimum balanced opening but one that is otherwise suitable, i.e. with A-x-x in partner's suit and no values in hearts, West passes. This should be played as an encouraging action. East's 3◇ forced the partnership to 3♠, so the quicker West arrives there the weaker he is. With an unsuitable hand he would have rebid 3♠. Suitably encouraged by West's pass, East is happy to bid the game.

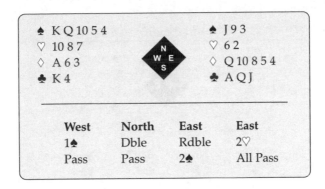

♠ K Q 10 5 4		♠ J 9 3	
♡ 10 8 7		♡ 6 2	
◇ A 6 3		◇ Q 10 8 5 4	
♣ K 4		♣ A Q J	

West	North	East	East
1♠	Dble	Rdble	2♡
Pass	Pass	2♠	All Pass

Here, with a weaker diamond suit and more values outside, there is no need to introduce the suit at all. A redouble and subsequent bid in spades describes the hand much better.

The Opponents Overcall

- Doubles are negative and will not generally have three-card support for opener unless at least invitational values are held.
- A 2NT bid is a matter for partnership discussion. Some like to play it as some different sort of fit-showing bid, while others are happy for it to be natural – after all, we do not always have a fit for partner and if a negative double makes some promises about four cards in unbid majors, we may be stuck without a good bid on a balanced hand with stoppers in the suit overcalled.
- Jumps in a new suit show fit. If the jump is below the level of three of the suit opened it shows only three-card support, while higher jumps guarantee a fit of four cards or more.
- A cue-bid of the suit overcalled shows four-card support and at least a limit raise. This can be a tricky position because opener does not know whether he is facing a game try or a stronger hand. With extra values should he simply bid game or make a waiting bid in case responder is stronger? One of the advantages of playing five-card majors is that when you know you have a 5-4 fit or better in a major you can afford to give up a natural 3NT. So, after a sequence such as: 1♠ – 2♡ – 3♡, a bid of 4♠ just shows a little extra but no slam interest at all; new suits at the four level show genuine slam interest facing a limit raise; and a bid of 3NT is somewhere in the middle – no real slam interest facing a limit raise but prepared to co-operate if responder is stronger.

Again, we need to look at some examples:

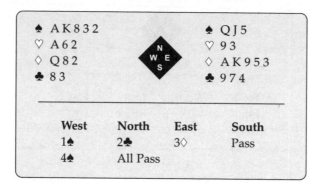

	♠ A K 8 3 2		♠ Q J 5
	♡ A 6 2		♡ 9 3
	◊ Q 8 2		◊ A K 9 5 3
	♣ 8 3		♣ 9 7 4

West	North	East	South
1♠	2♣	3◊	Pass
4♠	All Pass		

Although West has a minimum opener, the knowledge that East has a diamond suit and three-card spade support is enough for him to have a go at 4♠, a game that will make eleven tricks much of the time.

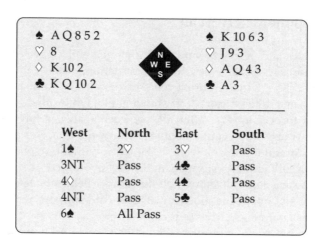

	♠ A Q 8 5 2		♠ K 10 6 3
	♡ 8		♡ J 9 3
	◊ K 10 2		◊ A Q 4 3
	♣ K Q 10 2		♣ A 3

West	North	East	South
1♠	2♡	3♡	Pass
3NT	Pass	4♣	Pass
4◊	Pass	4♠	Pass
4NT	Pass	5♣	Pass
6♠	All Pass		

East's 3♡ cue-bid initially shows just the values for a limit raise. West is not worth a slam try facing a limit raise, but will co-operate happily if East is stronger, so he rebids 3NT to show the medium-strength hand. East cue-bids 4♣ and West co-operates with 4◊. When it seems that East has no heart control, West's hand looks to be working well so he checks up via RKCB and bids the excellent slam.

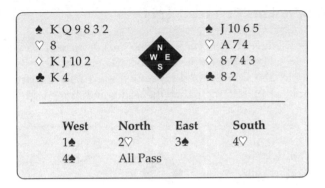

♠ K Q 9 8 3 2			♠ J 10 6 5
♡ 8			♡ A 7 4
◇ K J 10 2			◇ 8 7 4 3
♣ K 4			♣ 8 2

West	North	East	South
1♠	2♡	3♠	4♡
4♠	All Pass		

Knowledge that East has four-card support and not many values makes it easy for West to press on to 4♠ at any vulnerability. The worst that can happen is that 4♠ goes two down when it would surely be a good sacrifice. If South has the queen of diamonds and ace of clubs then 4♠ will make. If East had bid only 2♠, West would be unsure of the fourth trump, and it would not be nearly so clear for him to bid on, especially if he was vulnerable.

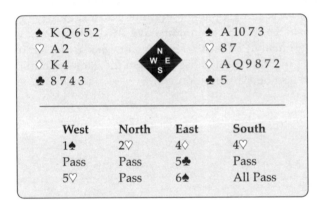

♣ K Q 6 5 2			♠ A 10 7 3
♡ A 2			♡ 8 7
◇ K 4			◇ A Q 9 8 7 2
♣ 8 7 4 3			♣ 5

West	North	East	South
1♠	2♡	4◇	4♡
Pass	Pass	5♣	Pass
5♡	Pass	6♠	All Pass

Over the 2♡ intervention, East's 4◇ shows a four-card spade fit. When South bids 4♡, West passes to show interest. Although he has a minimum opener, his hand is promising with the first-round heart control, good trumps and magic diamond holding. That is enough to persuade East to show his club control and West has enough for slam. He cue-bids his first-round heart control on the way to make sure they don't miss a grand slam when East has first-round club control.

The Opponents Overcall 1NT

Again, knowledge of five cards in the major opened can persuade responder to make a pre-emptive jump raise on some hands. Here, as over a double, 2NT can be used to show a good raise in partner's suit, surely a more useful treatment than the traditional strong two-suiter idea.

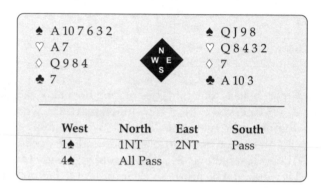

	♠ A 10 7 6 3 2		♠ Q J 9 8
	♡ A 7		♡ Q 8 4 3 2
	◇ Q 9 8 4		◇ 7
	♣ 7		♣ A 10 3

West	North	East	South
1♠	1NT	2NT	Pass
4♠	All Pass		

Over North's 1NT overcall, East does not want to do too much bidding in case West has an unsuitable minimum. So an aggressive action such as a raise to 4♠, which he might have tried over a 2◇ overcall, for example, seems out of order. He can show his serious game interest with a 2NT bid, and West is happy to bid the game on minimal values because of his good distribution.

QUIZ: BIDDING AFTER INTERVENTION

Partner opens 1♠ and the next hand doubles. What do you bid?

(1)	**(2)**	**(3)**
♠ K 7 6	♠ K 10 6	♠ K 10 5 4
♡ A 4	♡ 6 5	♡ K Q 10 8 3 2
◊ A 10 6 5	◊ 9 8 3	◊ 7 6
♣ 8 7 3 2	♣ A Q J 6 5	♣ 8

Partner opens 1♡ and the next hand overcalls 2♣. What do you bid?

(4)	**(5)**	**(6)**
♠ A 3	♠ A 7 6	♠ A K 6
♡ J 10 4	♡ J 10 4	♡ Q 6 5
◊ K Q J 7 6	◊ K 10 7 2	◊ J 10 9 7 6 2
♣ 9 8 4	♣ K 10 3	♣ 7

Partner opens 1♠ and the next hand overcalls 2♡. What do you bid?

(7)	**(8)**	**(9)**
♠ J 10 6 5 4	♠ K J 7 6	♠ J 8 7
♡ 7	♡ A 6 5	♡ A Q 10
◊ A Q 7 6 2	◊ K 10 8 7	◊ K J 10 7
♣ 9 8	♣ 8 7	♣ 10 9 4

Partner opens 1♡ and the next hand overcalls 1♠. What do you bid?

(10)	**(11)**	**(12)**
♠ J 8 7	♠ 8 7	♠ 9 8 7
♡ A Q 2	♡ Q 8 7 3	♡ K J 7
◊ J 5 4 3 2	◊ A 10 6 3	◊ 5 4
♣ 5 4	♣ 7 6 5	♣ A Q J 9 8

Partner opens 1♠ and the next hand doubles. What do you bid?

(1)	(2)	(3)
♠ K 7 6	♠ K 10 6	♠ K 10 5 4
♡ A 4	♡ 6 5	♡ K Q 10 8 3 2
◊ A 10 6 5	◊ 9 8 3	◊ 7 6
♣ 8 7 3 2	♣ A Q J 6 5	♣ 8

(1) Redouble. And bid 2♠ on the next round.

(2) 3♣. A three-card limit raise in spades with a club suit. Perfect.

(3) 4♡. This shows a good heart suit and four-card spade support. This hand does not have a great deal in terms of high-card points, but it is important to show the heart suit to help partner decide what to do if the opponents bid five of a minor.

Partner opens 1♡ and the next hand overcalls 2♣. What do you bid?

(4)	(5)	(6)
♠ A 3	♠ A 7 6	♠ A K 6
♡ J 10 4	♡ J 10 4	♡ Q 6 5
◊ K Q J 7 6	◊ K 10 7 2	◊ J 10 9 7 6 2
♣ 9 8 4	♣ K 10 3	♣ 7

(4) 3◊. A three-card limit heart raise with a diamond suit.

(5) 2NT. This is tricky. If the majors were the other way round and partner had opened 1♠, I would double despite not holding four hearts. If partner bid any number of hearts, I could convert to spades. But here if I double partner may bid 4♠, either freely or because the next hand raises clubs enthusiastically. That would leave me with nowhere to go. Instead I will start with a natural no-trump bid and hope to show my heart support later.

(6) Cue-bid 3♣, showing a four-card limit raise. The diamond suit is too weak to want to introduce. The overall suitability of the hand is such that the absence of the fourth trump probably will not matter.

Partner opens 1♠ and the next hand overcalls 2♡. What do you bid?

	(7)		(8)		(9)
♠	J 10 6 5 4	♠	K J 7 6	♠	J 8 7
♡	7	♡	A 6 5	♡	A Q 10
◇	A Q 7 6 2	◇	K 10 8 7	◇	K J 10 7
♣	9 8	♣	8 7	♣	10 9 4

(7) Bid 4◇, showing four-card or longer spade support and a decent diamond suit. You almost certainly will want to bid on to 4♠ over 4♡, but they may press on to 5♡ and you need to help partner judge what to do.

(8) Bid 3♡. A normal four-card limit raise.

(9) Bid 2NT. With three heart stoppers who cares about the spade support?

Partner opens 1♡ and the next hand overcalls 1♠. What do you bid?

	(10)		(11)		(12)
♠	J 8 7	♠	8 7	♠	9 8 7
♡	A Q 2	♡	Q 8 7 3	♡	K J 7
◇	J 5 4 3 2	◇	A 10 6 3	◇	5 4
♣	5 4	♣	7 6 5	♣	A Q J 9 8

(10) Bid 2♡, a normal simple raise.

(11) Bid 3♡, a pre-emptive raise.

(12) Bid 3♣, showing a three-card limit raise with a club suit.

WHAT HAVE WE LEARNED?

A   When the opponents come into the auction it is even more important to get across to partner how good your support is and whether you have concentrated values in a side suit.

B   If you can make a jump that is still below the level of three of the suit opened, then that shows the values for a three-level limit raise with only three trumps and a strongish side suit. It is not forcing to game, just to three of the suit opened.

C   When you have four-card (or longer) support and a good side-suit, then tell partner immediately with a jump to the four level in your side suit. Don't be too particular about how strong a hand you hold.

D   Don't jump around too enthusiastically when you have a balanced hand with good defence.

WHAT WENT WRONG?

In order to test your understanding of the material in this section, I will present you with a number of deals where the bidding sequence did not arrive in the optimum contract. It is up to you to study these sequences and decide how to apportion the blame.

(1)
♠ KQJ74
♡ 7
◇ AQJ63
♣ 96

♠ 1063
♡ 10962
◇ K104
♣ A103

West	North	East	South
1♠	Pass	1NT	Pass
2◇	Pass	2♠	All Pass

(2)
♠ K72
♡ KJ864
◇ 72
♣ J104

♠ QJ964
♡ A102
◇ KJ4
♣ Q3

West	North	East	South
		1♠	2◇
Dble	Pass	2NT	All Pass

(3)
♠ K3
♡ AQ1092
◇ QJ4
♣ KJ3

♠ J54
♡ 76
◇ A876
♣ Q1092

West	North	East	South
1♡	Pass	1NT	Pass
2NT	Pass	3NT	All Pass

(1)

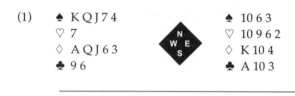

	♠ K Q J 7 4		♠ 10 6 3
	♡ 7		♡ 10 9 6 2
	◇ A Q J 6 3		◇ K 10 4
	♣ 9 6		♣ A 10 3

West	North	East	South
1♠	Pass	1NT	Pass
2◇	Pass	2♠	All Pass

East was at fault here. Although he has a normal 1NT response if playing four-card majors, playing five-card majors he should have raised spades immediately. This would have been more encouraging to West who would then have proceeded with a long-suit game try of 3◇. Now East, with his excellent diamond holding and outside ace, would have pressed on to game.

As it went, West was expecting only a doubleton in support of spades, making game in that suit extremely unlikely. And game in any other denomination was even less probable. No doubt when West passed 2♠ he was thinking it more likely he would go down than that he would have missed a game.

Correct auction:

West	North	East	South
1♠	Pass	2♠	Pass
3◇	Pass	4♠	All Pass

(2)

♠ K 7 2	♠ Q J 9 6 4
♡ K J 8 6 4	♡ A 10 2
◇ 7 2	◇ K J 4
♣ J 10 4	♣ Q 3

West	North	East	South
		1♠	2◇
Dble	Pass	2NT	All Pass

West was at fault here. He should have raised spades immediately. Had South not overcalled West would not have had any alternative and when the auction gets competitive it is even more important to show support for partner.

West hoped that, by doubling, his side would perhaps find a heart fit which might play better than spades. While there was some chance of this – if his partner had held four hearts for example – it was a luxury he could not afford. East's 2NT rebid was the most likely result of the double and now West could not show his spade support without vastly overstating his values.

Correct auction:

West	North	East	South
		1♠	2◇
2♠	All Pass		

(3)

	♠ K 3		♠ J 5 4
	♡ A Q 10 9 2		♡ 7 6
	◇ Q J 4		◇ A 8 7 6
	♣ K J 3		♣ Q 10 9 2

West	North	East	South
1♡	Pass	1NT	Pass
2NT	Pass	3NT	All Pass

Here West was at fault. Despite his five-card major he should have opened 1NT. As it went he did not know what to rebid when his partner responded 1NT. The range of East's 1NT is quite wide: about 6–11 high-card points. So West was right to worry about missing a game, but by raising to 2NT in this way he led his partner to believe that he was too strong for a 1NT opening bid. Consequently East placed his partner with 18 or 19 points so he made the slightly pushy raise to game.

If you have a balanced hand within your no-trump range, and do not open 1NT in the first place it can make life difficult later. Here, unless East made some sort of heart raise, West would have had no good rebid whatever East responded to 1♡.

Correct auction:

West	North	East	South
1NT	All Pass		

(4)   ♠ Q 4
      ♡ A Q 10 3 2   ♠ J 7 6 3 2
      ◇ K J 5   ♡ K
      ♣ A 4 3   ◇ A 4
                                  ♣ K Q 10 9 5

West	North	East	South
1♡	Pass	1♠	Pass
2♣	Pass	2◇	Pass
2NT	Pass	3♣	Pass
3NT	Pass	4◇	Pass
4♡	Pass	6♣	All Pass

(5)   ♠ A K 6 4 3
      ♡ A Q 2   ♠ 10 9 7 5
      ◇ 7   ♡ K J 10 4
      ♣ A 7 6 3   ◇ A 5 4
                                  ♣ 4 2

West	North	East	South
1♠	Pass	3♠	Pass
4♠	All Pass		

(6)   ♠ A 7 6 4 2
      ♡ 3   ♠ K Q 10 3
      ◇ A K 7 6 3 2   ♡ 7 6 2
      ♣ 7   ◇ 10 4
                                  ♣ A 9 8 4

West	North	East	South
1♠	3♡	3♠	4♡
4♠	All Pass		

(4)

	♠ Q 4		♠ J 7 6 3 2
	♡ A Q 10 3 2		♡ K
	◊ K J 5		◊ A 4
	♣ A 4 3		♣ K Q 10 9 5

West	North	East	South
1♡	Pass	1♠	Pass
2♣	Pass	2◊	Pass
2NT	Pass	3♣	Pass
3NT	Pass	4◊	Pass
4♡	Pass	6♣	All Pass

Again, West was at fault for not opening 1NT in the first place. On Hand (3) the problem was that he could not show the strength of his hand satisfactorily after opening 1♡. Another reason for opening 1NT whenever possible is that it makes the auction straightforward, as it immediately puts the partnership into familiar bidding territory.

Once West had failed to open 1NT he realised that he could not afford to rebid either 1NT or 2NT. He decided to temporise with a 2♣ rebid which got East rather excited. Too good for an immediate club raise, East first introduced fourth-suit forcing and then showed his club support. West's repeated no-trump rebids led East to think he was facing at most a singleton spade opposite, so he went on with a diamond cue-bid. When West at last showed some sign of life with a heart cue-bid, East bid the hopeless slam.

Correct auction:

West	North	East	South
1NT	Pass	2♡	Pass
2♠	Pass	3♣	Pass
3NT	All Pass		

ANSWERS TO WHAT WENT WRONG?

(5)   ♠ A K 6 4 3   ♠ 10 9 7 5
        ♡ A Q 2   ♡ K J 10 4
        ◇ 7   ◇ A 5 4
        ♣ A 7 6 3   ♣ 4 2

West	North	East	South
1♠	Pass	3♠	Pass
4♠	All Pass		

Here East was too strong for a pre-emptive spade raise. Players often place too high a value on the quality of the four-card support when supporting a five-card major. When partner's suit is likely to be only four cards long, then good trump support is an important asset, but when partner has a five-card suit it is more valuable to have your high cards outside. On this deal declarer is favourite to have no losers in spades so while the queen and/or jack of spades in the East hand would be an advantage it would only increase the odds of the slam making, not affect whether or not East-West wanted to bid it.

It is up to each partnership to define what is expected of a pre-emptive major-suit raise. My definition is that partner should expect a 4-4-3-2 distribution with four trumps, perhaps with an honour, and one certain trick outside.

Had East started with 3◇, West would have tried a natural(ish) and economical 3♡, thus greatly improving the East hand. East should raise to 4♡. His good heart fit is at least as important as his ace of diamonds which will be easier for him to show later or which West can locate via RKCB. As it is, West has to gamble on East's minor-suit length (North-South's silence suggests that East is shorter in clubs than diamonds).

Correct auction:

West	North	East	South
1♠	Pass	3◇	Pass
3♡	Pass	4♡	Pass
4NT	Pass	5◇	Pass
6♠	All Pass		

(6)

♠ A 7 6 4 2		♠ K Q 10 3
♡ 3	N	♡ 7 6 2
◊ A K 7 6 3 2	W E	◊ 10 4
♣ 7	S	♣ A 9 8 4

West	North	East	South
1♠	3♡	3♠	4♡
4♠	All Pass		

You will have guessed by now that I am always quick to spot auctions that go wrong after someone opens a hand with a five-card major when they have a six-card minor. There seem to be an infinite number of problems that can occur (yes, I do realise it works sometimes, or no-one would ever do it!).

Here in some ways the 1♠ opening made life easy because the fit was found immediately. However, North-South's actions made it hard for East-West to judge the strength of each other's hand. This was not entirely unexpected; West's exciting distribution made it more likely that the opponents would have exciting distribution too.

If West opens with a simple 1◊ and North overcalls the same 3♡, East has a clear take-out double. After 4♡ West would fancy his chances of slam but is 4NT Blackwood in this auction? Most would play it as offering some sort of choice in the minors, but if West then goes back to spades it surely shows a spade slam try, which East must accept with his good trumps and outside ace.

Correct auction:

West	North	East	South
1◊	3♡	Dble	4♡
4NT	Pass	5♣	Pass
5♠	Pass	6♠	All Pass

WHAT WENT WRONG?

(7)

♠ K Q 5 3 2		♠ J 10 7 4
♡ 7 6		♡ A 3
◊ 4		◊ A 9 2
♣ A K 8 4 2		♣ J 7 6 3

West	North	East	South
1♠	2♡	3♡	Pass
4♣	Pass	4◊	Pass
4♠	Pass	6♣	All Pass

(8)

♠ A 7 3		♠ J 9 4
♡ A K J 6 2		♡ Q 10 3
◊ 5		◊ K Q 10 4
♣ K Q J 9		♣ 7 6 2

West	North	East	South
1♡	Pass	2♡	Pass
3♣	Pass	3◊	Pass
4♡	All Pass		

(9)

♠ A K 7 6 2		♠ Q J 3
♡ 7 4		♡ A 9 2
◊ K Q 3 2		◊ J 10 4
♣ A 2		♣ K Q 6 3

West	North	East	South
1♠	Pass	2♣	Pass
2◊	Pass	2♡	Pass
3♣	Pass	3♠	Pass
4♠	All Pass		

(7) ♠ K Q 5 3 2   ♠ J 10 7 4
     ♡ 7 6   ♡ A 3
     ◇ 4      ◇ A 9 2
     ♣ A K 8 4 2   ♣ J 7 6 3

West	North	East	South
1♠	2♡	3♡	Pass
4♣	Pass	4◇	Pass
4♠	Pass	6♠	All Pass

West was wrong here. Although he has a nice hand he is not worth a slam try facing a normal limit raise, which is all East has shown. Had North not overcalled and East simply bid 3◇, surely West would have just bid 4♠. When West bid 4♣, East rightly thought that West had a real slam try and there was no stopping him.

West should have bid 3NT over 3♡. This is a conventional bid and shows slam interest only if East had the values for a game-force in the first place. Then East would have rebid 4♠ and the poor slam would have been avoided. However, maybe North will lead a diamond and maybe the queen of clubs will drop singleton or doubleton; sometimes bad bidding works out OK.

Correct auction:

West	North	East	South
1♠	2♡	3♡	Pass
3NT	Pass	4♠	All Pass

(8)

♠ A 7 3	♠ J 9 4
♡ A K J 6 2	♡ Q 10 3
◇ 5	◇ K Q 10 4
♣ K Q J 9	♣ 7 6 2

West	North	East	South
1♡	Pass	2♡	Pass
3♣	Pass	3◇	Pass
4♡	All Pass		

What was West thinking of here? Was he interested in a slam facing a simple raise? Or was he really considering not bidding game? All he succeeded in doing was telling the opponents to lead spades!

It is important not to forget that all the bids you make in an auction help the opponents with their opening lead and general defence. When you know where you are going you should get there as soon as possible – though sometimes there is scope for making some extra bids simply to try to mislead your opponents.

Correct auction:

West	North	East	South
1♡	Pass	2♡	Pass
4♡	All Pass		

ANSWERS TO WHAT WENT WRONG?

(9)

♠ A K 7 6 2		♠ Q J 3
♡ 7 4		♡ A 9 2
◇ K Q 3 2		◇ J 10 4
♣ A 2		♣ K Q 6 3

West	North	East	South
1♠	Pass	2♣	Pass
2◇	Pass	2♡	Pass
3♣	Pass	3♠	Pass
4♠	All Pass		

On this deal East got himself in a tangle because he never got around to showing West that he had real spade support. He should have bid 3NT over 1♠ which would have made the auction easy. He could also have bid a forcing 3♠ over 2◇. Remember, that because the initial two-level response is stronger than it would be in Acol, it makes sense to play most 'support' sequences, including jump preference, as forcing. This delayed support would have suggested a more distributional hand but would nevertheless at least have shown three spades. As it went it sounded to West as if East was merely trying to find the right game and couldn't play 3NT because of the lack of a satisfactory heart stopper. No doubt West thought his partner held something like: ♠Qx ♡Qxx ◇Axx ♣KQxxx when 4♠ is certainly where you want to be.

Correct auction:

West	North	East	South
1♠	Pass	3NT	Pass
4◇	Pass	4♡	Pass
5♣	Pass	6♠	All Pass

ITEMS RETURNED AFTER
LIBRARY
CLOSES ON DUE DATE ARE
CONSIDERED LATE

User ID: 29370001031164

Title: The easy guide to five-card majors
Item ID: 39370001913344
Date due: 2/15/2015,23:59

Title: More points schmoints!

Item ID: 39370001218769
Date due: 2/15/2015,23:59

Total checkouts for session:
2
Total checkouts:2

www.monroetwplibrary.org
Monroe Township Library
732-521-5000

PART II
OPENING WITHOUT
A FIVE-CARD MAJOR

What to Open?

We have covered the easy bit. Everyone in the world would play five-card majors if they were always dealt one. The problems associated with playing five-card majors arise when you do not hold one.

Obviously if your hand is within range for 1NT, then you do not have a problem. But you have to decide what you are going to open when it is outside that range. When I learned to play bridge such hands were often bid by opening one of the four-card suits with the intention of rebidding the other if necessary but that practice is frowned upon these days. It is generally considered desirable either to open or rebid no-trumps with a balanced hand (unless you find a fit with partner).

So, if you are playing a strong no-trump and are dealt either 12–14 or 18–19 points with one or more four-card majors but no five-card majors, the possible schemes are:

- Open 1◇ when you have four diamonds, otherwise open 1♣. The advantage of this is that your 1◇ opening is always natural.
- Always open 1♣ when you have a balanced hand with no five-card major. This means you only open 1◇ with at least a five-card suit (or an unbalanced hand – 4-4-4-1 hands will be discussed later).
- Open 1♣ when you are weaker than a 1NT opening, but 1◇ when you are stronger. This method is not in widespread use but I mention it because it is what I favour. Its disadvantages are that neither minor opening is natural, but on the other hand the 1♣ opening is not overloaded. It is much more frequently a weak balanced hand than anything else and it usually works OK for partner to assume that unless told otherwise.
- Open your better minor.

By far the most widespread of these methods worldwide is the 'better minor' approach, and that is the one I am going to look at in detail in this book.

Actually 'better minor' is usually something of a misnomer since the usual agreement is 'longer minor or 1♣ when you are 3-3 in the minors'. With 4-4 in the minors it is a matter of partnership agreement and there seems to be no consensus. In this book we will open our stronger minor when we are 4-4.

Playing 'better minor' the following hands would all open 1♣:

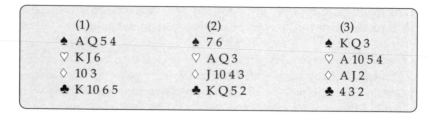

	(1)	(2)	(3)
♠	A Q 5 4	7 6	K Q 3
♡	K J 6	A Q 3	A 10 5 4
◊	10 3	J 10 4 3	A J 2
♣	K 10 6 5	K Q 5 2	4 3 2

However, these would open 1◊:

	(4)	(5)	(6)
♠	A 4 3	A 10 6 5	A 3
♡	K 7 6 5	K 10 5 4	K Q 4
◊	A Q 5 4	7 3 2	K 10 8 7
♣	6 5	A Q	J 7 6 3

Differences in Responding Strategy

Majors before Minors

The main difference in responding style compared with Acol is that it becomes very much more important to bid your majors immediately. If you respond 1◇ to partner's opening 1♣, he will rebid 1NT when he has a balanced 12–14 points (unless he has a fit with you), and you do not want to miss a 4-4 major-suit fit. So the general rule is that unless you have game-forcing values after a 1♣ opening bid you should bypass diamonds in favour of responding in a four-card major. (This agreement is known as Walsh in the US.) You should also prefer to respond in a four-card major than to raise partner's minor even with five-card support (this is a practice also generally adopted – very wrongly in my view – when playing Acol).

Let's look at a few responding hands.

Suppose you hold this hand after partner opens 1♣:

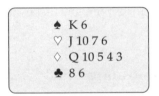

```
♠ K 6
♡ J 10 7 6
◇ Q 10 5 4 3
♣ 8 6
```

If you were playing Acol there would be little to lose by responding 1◇. If partner has four hearts he will rebid them over 1◇ and the fit will be found. There is no chance that partner is 4-4 in hearts and clubs because then he would have opened 1♡.

However, playing our system, if you respond 1◇ partner will rebid 1NT on most balanced hands (though he will occasionally raise diamonds), even with four hearts. As you do not have the values to proceed over the 1NT rebid the heart fit will be lost. The ability to find 4-4 major-suit fits at part-score level when opener has the most frequent opening hand-type (a balanced hand in the 12–14 range) is one of the advantages our system has over Acol, so it would be a pity to lose that edge.

Now let's look at a different hand:

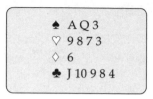

$\spadesuit$ A Q 3
$\heartsuit$ 9 8 7 3
$\diamondsuit$ 6
$\clubsuit$ J 10 9 8 4

Again suppose partner opens 1$\clubsuit$. In my view if you were playing Acol you should raise clubs immediately. Although beginners are taught to respond 1$\heartsuit$, that does not make sense within modern Acol where the four-card major is opened wherever possible. The only time opener will have four hearts is when he has five clubs. If such a double fit does exist then most of the time the opponents will enter the auction and it is more important that opener learns of the five-card club support than some scrappy four-card major.

However, when playing five-card majors it is a different matter. Opener is quite likely to hold only three clubs, and may well hold four hearts. Now it is important to investigate the major-suit fit.

Responding in No-trumps

- A 1NT response to a 'better minor' opening is much the same as over an Acol opening. It shows a balanced hand with about 7–10 points and denies a four-card major.
- A 2NT response to a 'better minor' opening is natural, showing a balanced hand with 11–12 points and no four-card major.
- A 3NT response to a 'better minor' opening is natural, showing a balanced hand with 13–15 points and no four-card major

QUIZ:
DIFFERENCES IN RESPONDING STRATEGY

Partner opens 1♣. What would you respond with the following hands?

(1)	(2)	(3)
♠ J 9 8 3	♠ 5 4 3 2	♠ A Q 2
♡ A 6 2	♡ 6 5	♡ 7 6 5 2
◊ K Q J 6 4	◊ K J 10 8 7 6	◊ K 6 5
♣ 7	♣ 3	♣ J 6 4

(4)	(5)	(6)
♠ K J 5	♠ 5 4 3	♠ K J 6
♡ Q 9 5	♡ A 6 5	♡ A 10 3
◊ J 8 7 5	◊ A 5 4 2	◊ Q 10 4 3
♣ Q 9 3	♣ J 6 2	♣ J 4 3

(7)	(8)	(9)
♠ J 9 8 3	♠ Q 4 3 2	♠ 5 4 3 2
♡ A 7	♡ 6 5 2	♡ 6 5 2
◊ A K J 6 5	◊ 7	◊ 7
♣ Q 2	♣ A Q 9 8 4	♣ A Q 10 9 8

Partner opens 1◊. What would you respond with the following hands?

(10)	(11)	(12)
♠ A Q 2	♠ 6	♠ K Q 10 5
♡ 8 7 3 2	♡ 8 7 3 2	♡ Q 7 4
◊ K J 6 2	◊ K J 10 6 2	◊ 7
♣ 9 2	♣ Q 6 3	♣ A K 8 7 3

Partner opens 1♣. What would you respond with the following hands?

(1)	(2)	(3)
♠ J 9 8 3	♠ 5 4 3 2	♠ A Q 2
♡ A 6 2	♡ 6 5	♡ 7 6 5 2
◇ K Q J 6 4	◇ K J 10 8 7 6	◇ K 6 5
♣ 7	♣ 3	♣ J 6 4

(1) 1♠. Without the values for a game-force, start by investigating the major-suit fit.

(2) 1◇. OK, I've finally given in. With such a weak one-bid hand I prefer to bid my long suit. But this bid could easily backfire because partner might rebid 2NT to show 18–19 and I would not be able to investigate for a 4-4 spade fit without overstating my values (partner would expect opening-bid values as soon as he discovered I had four spades).

(3) Bid 1♡. It does not matter how weak your four-card major, it is still best to respond in it.

(4)	(5)	(6)
♠ K J 5	♠ 5 4 3	♠ K J 6
♡ Q 9 5	♡ A 6 5	♡ A 10 3
◇ J 8 7 5	◇ A 5 4 2	◇ Q 10 4 3
♣ Q 9 3	♣ J 6 2	♣ J 4 3

(4) Here bid 1NT. This does not promise four clubs (as many Acol players would expect), but does deny a four-card major.

(5) Bid 1◇. Although you have the values and distribution for a 1NT response, your lack of tenaces suggests that it would be better for partner to be declarer.

(6) Bid 2NT. After a minor-suit opening this is natural, showing 11–12 points and denying a four-card major.

	(7)	**(8)**	**(9)**
♠	J 9 8 3	Q 4 3 2	5 4 3 2
♡	A 7	6 5 2	6 5 2
◊	A K J 6 5	7	7
♣	Q 2	A Q 9 8 4	A Q 10 9 8

(7) Bid 1◊. With the values for a game-force, there is no reason to do other than bid your hand naturally, long suit first.

(8) Bid 1♠. When you have such good clubs it is overwhelmingly likely that partner has a weak no-trump hand-type. First investigate the spade fit and if you don't have one trust that partner has decent diamonds.

(9) Again, it could work best to bid 1♠, but raising clubs directly will make it easier for partner to compete if the opponents come in with a red suit. Here I would raise to 2♣.

Partner opens 1◊. What would you respond on the following hands?

	(10)	**(11)**	**(12)**
♠	A Q 2	6	K Q 10 5
♡	8 7 3 2	8 7 3 2	Q 7 4
◊	K J 6 2	K J 10 6 2	7
♣	9 2	Q 6 3	A K 8 7 3

(10) Respond 1♡. If partner makes a rebid that promises a real diamond suit you can support him later.

(11) Here I would raise directly to 2◊. It looks as if the opponents are about to bid spades and raising to 2◊ will make it easier for partner to compete when that is the right thing to do.

(12) Bid 2♣. With game-forcing values, bid your suits in natural order.

WHAT HAVE WE LEARNED?

A   Generally speaking when partner opens 1♣ you should respond in a four-card major ahead of either bidding diamonds or raising partner's minor unless you have game-forcing values.

B   When you have game-forcing values start by bidding your minor. However, when your minor is the suit opened you cannot do this (though we will look at *inverted minor-suit raises*, a convention that enables you to do this, later on) and have to start with your major in any event.

C   When you have a really weak hand with a very weak four-card major and a good five-card minor it can work well to bid the minor (especially if it means raising partner) because it makes it easier for partner to compete if the opponents enter the auction.

D   Whether you respond 1◊ or 1NT to a 1♣ opening with a balanced hand should depend on whether or not you have tenaces; when you have tenaces ensure you become declarer by bidding 1NT, otherwise respond 1◊ and let partner rebid 1NT.

The Continuing Auction

What to Rebid?

So, you have opened a 'better minor' and partner responds in a major. It feels as if it should be easy:

- With 12–14 points and four-card support, raise partner.
- With 12–14 points and a balanced hand without four-card support, rebid 1NT.
- With a balanced hand too strong to open 1NT, rebid 2NT or make a jump or double jump raise in partner's suit.

That sounds straightforward but there are some problem hands. Let's look at a few of them.

Suppose you have a balanced hand with a four-card spade suit and partner responds 1♡ to your opening one of a minor. Should you rebid 1♠ or 1NT? The problem with rebidding in no-trumps is that if partner has a weakish hand with 4-4 or 4-5 in the majors, the spade fit will be lost. The problem with rebidding 1♠ is that partner will not know that you have a balanced hand.

My recommendation is a compromise: rebid 1♠ when you have four cards in the minor you opened, but rebid 1NT when you are 4-3-3-3.

(1)	(2)	(3)
♠ A J 10 4	♠ K Q 10 3	♠ Q 10 4 3
♡ Q 6	♡ K 7 2	♡ J 10 7
◇ 7 6 3	◇ J 10 5 4	◇ A K 5
♣ A J 7 4	♣ K 5	♣ K 10 3

With Hand (1), open 1♣. If partner responds 1◇ rebid 1NT; partner will bid again if he has four spades (Walsh, see page 79). However, if he responds 1♡ rebid 1♠ to make sure you don't miss a 4-4 spade fit. With Hand (2) open 1◇ and rebid 1♠ over 1♡. However, with Hand (3) open 1♣ and rebid 1NT over 1♡.

Now let's look at a different kind of problem. Suppose you hold the following hand:

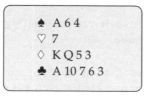

♠ A 6 4
♡ 7
♢ K Q 5 3
♣ A 10 7 6 3

You open 1♣ and partner responds 1♠. What do you rebid?

It seems silly to rebid 2♣, a suit in which partner may have a singleton, when you know you have at least a seven-card spade fit. However, if you are going to raise to 2♠ on this deal then such a raise cannot promise four-card support and partner has to proceed a little carefully. He should not assume you have four-card support for a raise; three-card support with a singleton on the side is perfectly acceptable.

Now suppose that instead of responding 1♠ partner responds 1♡. What now? If 1NT promises a balanced hand then there is no alternative to rebidding 2♣, again a suit in which partner may be very short. And indeed many players would do this. But there is another school of thought that allows a 1NT rebid to include a singleton in partner's suit. This is an important matter for partnerships to decide, but I would go with the latter view. I would allow the singleton in partner's suit.

Although a 1NT rebid may contain a singleton in partner's suit, the same is not the case with a 2NT rebid, which must always be a balanced hand of 18–19 points.

Other problems can occur with the sequence 1♣ – 1♠ – 3♠ or 1♣ – 1♠ – 4♠. Are these sequences consistent with a balanced 18–19 points, or can opener be lighter with more distribution? The simple approach is the following:

- With 18–19 points and a balanced hand or perhaps a little lighter with five clubs and four spades but no singleton, raise to 4♠ (though this can lead to a pretty poor game with a 4-3-3-3 18-count facing some minimum responding hands).
- With 14–16 points and fair distribution raise to 3♠.
- With 17–19 points and a singleton, make a splinter bid (i.e. make a jump rebid in your singleton.

Bidding after Opener Raises Responder's Suit

After opener makes a jump raise of responder's suit, there is little to be said. Responder either bids on or does not, perhaps cue-bidding in a search for slam. However, after a simple raise responder may wish to investigate the hand more scientifically. He may like to ascertain for certain that opener has four-card support, or may wish to look for a slam.

Some pairs are happy to do all this naturally, but there is much to be said for having the agreement that a 2NT rebid by responder is forcing, though will usually be a balanced hand. Now if opener has only three-card support he can rebid 3♣, otherwise he makes his most natural bid, or he can jump to show a singleton with four-card support.

Let's look at some examples:

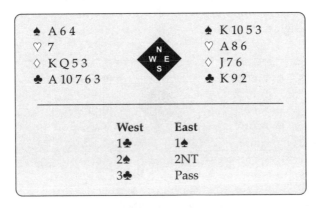

	♠ A 6 4		♠ K 10 5 3
	♡ 7		♡ A 8 6
	◇ K Q 5 3		◇ J 7 6
	♣ A 10 7 6 3		♣ K 9 2

West	East
1♣	1♠
2♠	2NT
3♣	Pass

East had nothing to spare for his 2NT bid in any event. Hearing that West had only three spades and therefore a singleton in one of the red suits was enough to put him off either 3NT or 4♠ as a final resting place, so the auction stopped in the safe club part-score.

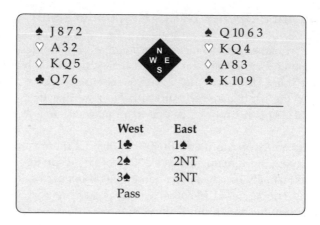

♠ J 8 7 2	♠ Q 10 6 3
♡ A 3 2	♡ K Q 4
◇ K Q 5	◇ A 8 3
♣ Q 7 6	♣ K 10 9

West	East
1♣	1♠
2♠	2NT
3♠	3NT
Pass	

West has a truly dreadful hand, so signs off in 3♠ over 2NT. But East's purpose was always trying to decide whether 4♠ or 3NT would be the right game so he continues with 3NT to show his 4-3-3-3 distribution. West is delighted to pass.

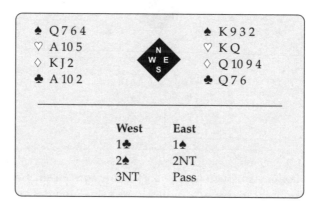

♠ Q 7 6 4	♠ K 9 3 2
♡ A 10 5	♡ K Q
◇ K J 2	◇ Q 10 9 4
♣ A 10 2	♣ Q 7 6

West	East
1♣	1♠
2♠	2NT
3NT	Pass

This time West is maximum in terms of high-card points but has the same unexciting 4-3-3-3 distribution. He should suggest this by raising 2NT to 3NT. He must have four spades (or he would have rebid 3♣) and the only reason for raising no-trumps must be that he is completely balanced. East's strong doubleton heart honour should persuade him to opt for the no-trump game, a much better proposition on the two combined hands above than the alternative spade game.

```
        ♠ Q J 6 5                    ♠ A K 10 3
        ♡ A K 6 5          N         ♡ Q 4
        ◇ A 3           W     E      ◇ 9 8 7 2
        ♣ 8 7 6            S         ♣ A K 2


                    West      East
                    1♣        1♠
                    2♠        2NT
                    3♡        4♣
                    4◇        4NT
                    5♠        6♠
                    Pass
```

With a maximum and a good heart suit, West bids 3♡ over 2NT. This is
good news for East. He expects West's distribution to be what it is (with
4-4-3-2 he would have opened 1◇). So he presses on with a club cue-bid
and then uses RKCB when West shows a diamond control. Aggressive
bidding, yes, but based on good inferences.

Bidding after Opener Rebids 1NT

After the 12–14 1NT rebid responder needs to find out distributional
information from opener and also needs to be able to bid weak,
invitational and strong hands of his own. One of the hand-types we have
to deal with, remember, is when responder has responded one of a major
but has a longer diamond suit. Here are some of the available schemes:

- New minor forcing. This is more or less what it says it is: if 1♣ has
  been opened then 2♣ after the 1NT rebid would be natural and
  weak, while a 2◇ rebid is the enquiry; if 1◇ has been opened then
  it is the other way around.
- 2♣ and 2◇ are both artificial bids of some sort showing different
  hand-types. A simple method is to use 2♣ as a sign-off with weak
  hands and 2◇ as a game-forcing enquiry, which frees all other bids
  to be natural and invitational. Over 2♣ opener is forced to rebid 2◇
  which responder may pass or sign off in another suit. This also
  allows responder to show varying strengths of canapé hand with
  a four-card major and a long minor. (In the US it is common for 2♣
  to show invitational hands and 2♡/2♠ to be weak.)

- Checkback. This is the simplest of them all. A 2♣ bid over 1NT (and 3♣ over a 2NT rebid) simply asks opener about his major-suit holdings. After 1♣ – 1♡ – 1NT – 2♣, for example, 2♡ would show three hearts, 2♠ would show four spades and deny three hearts, while 2◇ would be bid on any other hand. Rebids of 2NT or higher are unusual, but natural and descriptive. Checkback is the convention in most widespread use and is what we will look at here.

One of the more basic questions for partnerships to answer is what continuations are forcing and what are not. For example, what is the difference between the sequence 1♣ – 1♠ – 1NT – 3♡ and 1♣ – 1♠ – 1NT – 2♣ – 2◇ – 3♡? The simple rule is that to bid Checkback and then a new suit is forcing, while to jump in a suit initially is invitational.

At least in the sequence above it is fairly clear that if 1♣ – 1♠ – 1NT – 3♡ is invitational it should show two five-card suits, for with a 5-4 hand responder could use Checkback and sign off in 2NT if no eight-card major-suit fit were found. But what of the sequence 1♣ – 1♠ – 1NT – 3◇? Does this also show 5-5 or could responder be trying to show an invitational hand with 4-5 or 4-6 distribution? That is something for each individual partnership to decide but I would go for the latter. If responder has an invitational 5-5 hand then he can find out whether or not partner has three-card support for his major; if not he has to choose between signing off in the major or inviting via 2NT.

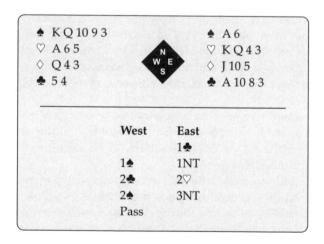

	♠ K Q 10 9 3		♠ A 6
	♡ A 6 5	N W E S	♡ K Q 4 3
	◇ Q 4 3		◇ J 10 5
	♣ 5 4		♣ A 10 8 3

West	East
	1♣
1♠	1NT
2♣	2♡
2♠	3NT
Pass	

West is minimum for Checkback and over East's 2♡ bids 2♠ showing a good five-card suit and invitational values. East is happy to bid 3NT with his super-maximum.

Easy Guide to Five-Card Majors

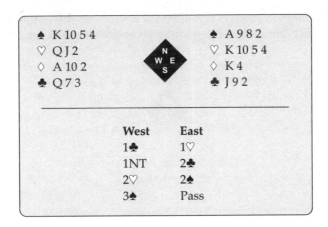

♠ K 10 5 4   ♠ A 9 8 2
♡ Q J 2   ♡ K 10 5 4
◇ A 10 2   ◇ K 4
♣ Q 7 3   ♣ J 9 2

West	East
1♣	1♡
1NT	2♣
2♡	2♠
3♠	Pass

If West rebids 1NT with 4-3-3-3 distribution, the fit may be lost if East passes 1NT, but if East is strong enough to use Checkback the fit can be found later. Here West responds 2♡ to Checkback, because that is his lowest feature. East now bids his four-card spade suit. With a minimum hand and four spades, West makes a non-forcing raise to 3♠ which on this occasion East passes. If West were stronger he could jump to 4♠, or else jump in a new suit at the four level as a cue-bid.

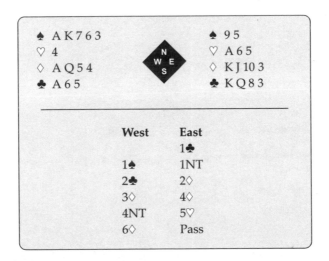

♠ A K 7 6 3   ♠ 9 5
♡ 4   ♡ A 6 5
◇ A Q 5 4   ◇ K J 10 3
♣ A 6 5   ♣ K Q 8 3

West	East
	1♣
1♠	1NT
2♣	2◇
3◇	4◇
4NT	5♡
6◇	Pass

West's main reason for using Checkback here was to create a forcing sequence. Over the 2◇ response he bid a forcing 3◇, showing slam interest (otherwise why introduce the minor suit). East's hand was suitable so he raised diamonds and West was happy to use RKCB to locate the missing 'aces'. It was positively good news that East held only a doubleton spade. On the actual two hands the grand slam is a fair contract, but only because of East's good diamond intermediates.

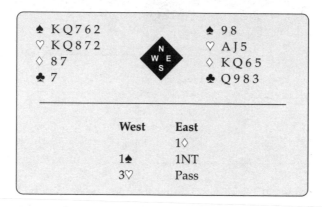

	♠ KQ762		♠ 98
	♡ KQ872		♡ AJ5
	◇ 87		◇ KQ65
	♣ 7		♣ Q983

West	East
	1◇
1♠	1NT
3♡	Pass

After the 1NT rebid West's hand is well suited to a jump to 3♡, showing invitational values and 5-5 distribution. With a minimum, only three-card heart support, no outside ace and no supporting honour in spades, East is happy to pass. 4♡ may make but it is not with the odds.

Choose your next bid on the following hands after the auctions given below:

(1)
♠ Q 10 5 4
♡ A 5
◇ K Q J 6
♣ 7 6 3

1◇	1♠
2♠	2NT
?	

(2)
♠ A 8 7 3
♡ 7 6
◇ K Q 10 8 7 2
♣ 6

1♣	1♠
1NT	?

(3)
♠ K Q J 7 6
♡ 6
◇ A 10 7 6 3
♣ 8 7

1♣	1♠
1NT	?

(4)
♠ 8 7
♡ K Q J 7 6 3
◇ A 8 6
♣ 6 2

1♣	1♡
1NT	?

(5)
♠ K Q 5 4
♡ A 5 4
◇ 8
♣ K Q 8 7 2

1♣	1♠
?	

(6)
♠ A K 8 4
♡ K 7
◇ K J 7 6
♣ A 10 5

1◇	1♠
?	

(7)
♠ K 10 6 5
♡ K 7 6
◇ A Q 6 4
♣ Q 7

1♣	1♠
2♠	?

(8)
♠ Q
♡ K J 10 4
◇ A Q 6
♣ J 8 7 4 3

1♣	1♠
?	

(9)
♠ K J 7 6
♡ A Q 6 5
◇ Q 5 4
♣ 9 7

1♣	1♡
1NT	?

Choose your next bid on the following hands after the auctions given below:

	(1)		(2)		(3)
♠	Q 10 5 4	♠	A 8 7 3	♠	K Q J 7 6
♡	A 5	♡	7 6	♡	6
◇	K Q J 6	◇	K Q 10 8 7 2	◇	A 10 7 6 3
♣	7 6 3	♣	6	♣	8 7

(1)		(2)		(3)	
1◇	1♠	1♣	1♠	1♣	1♠
2♠	2NT	1NT	?	1NT	?
?					

(1)   Bid 3♡. Although you are minimum in terms of high-card points, you have a nice 12-count. You have 4-4-3-2 distribution which is hugely superior to 4-3-3-3, and you have a chunky concentrated diamond suit, along with an outside ace and respectable trumps. While actually bidding game would be pushing it a bit, there is no need to sign off in 3♠. Instead tell partner of your heart feature and leave it up to him. 3◇ would be non-forcing, showing a five-card suit with only three spades.

(2)   Bid 3◇. Acol players would have responded diamonds in the first place and now we know partner doesn't have four spades that is what we wish we had done too. However, 3◇ on the second round shows invitational values with a good diamond suit and seems to express the hand well (this does not show five spades, see page 90). Don't worry that the hand is not strong enough in terms of points to invite game facing a weak no-trump. As long as partner has a diamond honour there are very good chances of making game.

(3)   Bid 2♣. If you bid 3◇ on the previous hand it cannot be the right bid on this one. Start with 2♣. If partner bids 2♠ raise him to 3♠, inviting him to go on with a suitable-looking hand. If he bids 2◇ or 2♡ content yourself with 2♠. This shows invitational values with a decent five-card suit. Perhaps he will bid on with 2NT and now you can introduce your diamonds.

(4)	(5)	(6)
♠ 8 7	♠ K Q 5 4	♠ A K 8 4
♡ K Q J 7 6 3	♡ A 5 4	♡ K 7
◇ A 8 6	◇ 8	◇ K J 7 6
♣ 6 2	♣ K Q 8 7 2	♣ A 10 5
1♣ 1♡	1♣ 1♠	1◇ 1♠
1NT ?	?	?

(4) Bid 3♡. This is invitational and shows a decent six-card suit. With a stronger hand you might bid 2♣ first and then rebid 3♡, forcing, either to suggest slam interest, or to offer partner a choice of games.

(5) Bid 3♠. Although you have only 14 high-card points this hand has a lot of potential. If you bid only 2♠ partner will think you have a weak no-trump with four-card spade support. He will pass most of the time that he has 10 or fewer points and that could easily lead to a missed game. Unless you jump to 3♠ he will not even know that you have a club suit.

(6) Bid 4♠. If you had a distributional hand you would either jump to 3♠ or else make a splinter bid (showing about 17–19 points with a club suit, at least four-card support for partner and a singleton). When you jump directly to game partner knows that you do not have a singleton and therefore must have an awful lot of high cards. He should know immediately whether there are any prospects of slam.

	(7)		(8)		(9)
♠	K 10 6 5	♠	Q	♠	K J 7 6
♡	K 7 6	♡	K J 10 4	♡	A Q 6 5
◇	A Q 6 4	◇	A Q 6	◇	Q 5 4
♣	Q 7	♣	J 8 7 4 3	♣	9 7

1♣	1♠	1♣	1♠	1♣	1♡
2♠	?	?		1NT	?

(7) Bid 2NT. It would be a mistake to jump straight to 4♠ because partner might have only three-card support. A 4-3 fit is often a good idea but the four-card trump suit needs to be stronger than the one you have here. If partner rebids 3♣, bid 3◇ showing values in the suit. If partner's distribution is 3-4-1-5 he will bid 3NT now. If his singleton is in hearts you will just have to risk the 4-3 spade fit anyway.

(8) I know many people like to have a balanced hand when they rebid no-trumps but sometimes it is just the least of all evils. Surely on this hand-type it is better to rebid 1NT than 2♣. You could imagine playing in 2♣ going down when 3NT or even 4♡ was cold. If partner insists on spades it will not necessarily be a disaster.

(9) Bid 2♣. Remember that partner could still hold a four-card spade suit. It would be careless not to check up on it. If partner bids 2◇ rebid a non-forcing 2NT; if he bids 2♡ you can bid 2♠ (he may be 4-3-2-4) without committing your side to game.

QUIZ: MORE ON THE CONTINUING AUCTION

Choose your next bid on the following hands after the auctions given below and give an example hand for partner that fits with his bidding.

(1)
♠ A Q 8 7 4
♡ 7
♢ K 7 6
♣ A K J 7

1♢	1♠
1NT	2♣
2♢	3♣
3♢	?

(2)
♠ A K 4
♡ A 7 6
♢ Q 10 7
♣ J 10 7 3

1♣	1♡
1NT	3♡
?	

(3)
♠ 9 8 7 5
♡ A Q 6
♢ K J 4
♣ A 10 5

1♣	1♠
2♠	2NT
?	

(4)
♠ A K 5
♡ 7 5 4 2
♢ 7
♣ A Q 10 7 6

1♣	1♠
2♠	2NT
3♣	3♢
?	

(5)
♠ Q 8 7 5 4
♡ K 10 3
♢ A J 6
♣ J 7

1♣	1♠
1NT	?

(6)
♠ A K 8 7 4
♡ 8
♢ A K Q 5 4
♣ A 3

1♣	1♠
1NT	2♣
2♢	

(7)
♠ K 6 5 4
♡ 7 6
♢ A 10 7 6 3 2
♣ 6

1♣	1♠
1NT	?

(8)
♠ K Q 10 6
♡ A Q 10 8 7
♢ 7 6
♣ 9 7

1♣	1♡
1NT	?

(9)
♠ A Q 5 4
♡ K J 6
♢ A 5
♣ K J 5 4

1♣	1♠
1NT	2♣
2♠	?

Choose your next bid on the following hands after the auctions given below and give an example hand for partner that fits with his bidding.

	(1)		(2)		(3)
♠	A Q 8 7 4	♠	A K 4	♠	9 8 7 5
♡	7	♡	A 7 6	♡	A Q 6
◇	K 7 6	◇	Q 10 7	◇	K J 4
♣	A K J 7	♣	J 10 7 3	♣	A 10 5

(1)		(2)		(3)	
1◇	1♠	1♣	1♡	1♣	1♠
1NT	2♣	1NT	3♡	2♠	2NT
2♠	3♣	?		?	
3◇	?				

(1) Bid 4◇. It seems as if partner is making all the right noises. He has three-card spade support, and now he is showing good diamonds. 4◇ shows your 5-1-3-4 distribution and should persuade him to proceed if he has no wasted values in hearts.

> ♠ K 9 6
> ♡ J 9 6
> ◇ A Q 5 4
> ♣ Q 6 5

(2) Bid 3NT. Partner has shown a long good heart suit and invitational values. You can almost count nine tricks: six hearts, two top spades and an ace with partner. There may be more problems in 4♡.

> ♠ 8 7
> ♡ K Q J 9 4 3
> ◇ A 8
> ♣ 8 6 2

(3) Bid 3NT. Partner's 2NT is forcing. You are maximum in high cards for your 2♠ raise but have poor trumps and the worst possible distribution. 3NT shows your 4-3-3-3 distribution and allows partner to pass when his distribution is the same as yours.

> ♠ A Q 10 3
> ♡ K 7 2
> ◇ Q 6 5
> ♣ J 3 2

(4)	(5)	(6)
♠ A K 5	♠ Q 8 7 5 4	♠ A K 8 7 4
♡ 7 5 4 2	♡ K 10 3	♡ 8
◇ 7	◇ A J 6	◇ A K Q 5 4
♣ A Q 10 7 6	♣ J 7	♣ A 3

1♣	1♠	1♣	1♠	1♣	1♠
2♠	2NT	1NT	?	1NT	2♣
3♣	3◇			2◇	?
?					

(4)   3♠. Your 3♣ bid said you had only three spades, in which case you must have a singleton in a red suit. Partner is asking you to bid 3NT when you have a singleton diamond and a heart stopper. You have the singleton diamond but no heart stopper. If you had a singleton heart you would bid at the four level so your choice now is between 3♡ and 3♠. With such good spades and nothing at all in hearts, 3♠ is the better choice. You have already denied a four-card spade suit. Facing the hand above, 4♠ is far from cold but it is the best game available.

> ♠ Q J 7 6
> ♡ 8 6
> ◇ K Q 10 4
> ♣ K J 5

(5)   Bid 2NT. This doesn't look like a hand for suit play even if partner does have three-card spade support. If he really likes spades, i.e. has three-card support and a small doubleton somewhere, he can always bid 3♠ over 2NT.

> ♠ K J 2
> ♡ Q 9 4 2
> ◇ K 5
> ♣ A 10 9 3

(6)   Bid 4◇. There is nothing wrong with a simple 3◇, as this is certainly forcing (new suit after Checkback), but bidding 4◇ tells partner immediately of your good 5-5 and slam interest. A grand slam could easily be on.

> ♠ Q 5
> ♡ A J 4
> ◇ J 10 8
> ♣ K J 7 6 4

(7)	**(8)**	**(9)**
♠ K 6 5 4	♠ K Q 10 6	♠ A Q 5 4
♡ 7 6	♡ A Q 10 8 7	♡ K J 6
◇ A 10 7 6 3 2	◇ 7 6	◇ A 5
♣ 6	♣ 9 7	♣ K J 5 4

1♣	1♠	1♣	1♡	1♣	1♠
1NT	?	1NT	?	1NT	2♣
				2♠	?

(7) Bid 2◇. You need to agree with your partner what your distribution should be for this bid. Since partner has already failed to raise spades it seems more useful to be able to bid a long suit elsewhere rather than bid again with five spades and four diamonds. I like to play that 2◇ here guarantees a five-card suit and partner will usually pass.

> ♠ A 7 3
> ♡ Q 5 3 2
> ◇ K Q 5
> ♣ Q 7 5

(8) Bid 2♠. Natural and non-forcing (no Checkback) but must show extra values because it forces preference at the three level. If you had only four hearts you would use Checkback and bid 2♠ if partner bid 2♡.

> ♠ A J 5 4
> ♡ K 9 2
> ◇ A 9 4
> ♣ J 8 2

(9) Bid 3♣. Maybe 3NT is the limit but partner could quite easily have a five-card club suit on this auction when 6♣ could easily be on. Showing your four-card club suit (forcing as it is effectively a new suit) allows partner to get excited if he so chooses.

> ♠ K 8 3
> ♡ A 4
> ◇ 10 9 4
> ♣ A Q 7 6 2

WHAT HAVE WE LEARNED?

A   If you open a prepared minor and partner responds in a major, to raise him you need either four-card support or three-card support and a side-suit singleton.

B   If you open 1♣ and partner responds 1◇, always rebid 1NT (or raise diamonds) with a balanced hand because partner would not respond 1◇ with a four-card major unless he intended to bid over 1NT. However, if he responds 1♡ rebid 1NT with four spades only if you are 4-3-3-3; if you have four cards in the suit you opened rebid 1♠.

C   Although a 1NT rebid is usually based on a balanced hand, sometimes you have a 5-4-3-1 with a singleton in partner's suit where there is really no sensible alternative. It is better to rebid 1NT with a singleton in partner's suit than to rebid a poor five-card suit.

D   A jump rebid of 2NT is always based on a balanced hand, i.e. no singleton.

E   After opener raises responder's major a 2NT rebid is best played as forcing for one round.

F   After a 1NT rebid 2♣ is best played as Checkback. Unless you go through Checkback, nothing is forcing. Checkback followed by a new suit at the two level is forcing for one round, while a new suit at the three level is forcing to game (three of the minor opened also counts as a new suit).

Opening with 4-4-4-1 Hands

Oh, how I hate 4-4-4-1 hands! They are neither one thing nor the other, neither fish nor fowl, neither balanced nor distributional! Give me 5-4-3-1 or 4-4-3-2 any day. Still, like anyone else in the world, roughly 3% of the time I am dealt a 4-4-4-1 hand. And roughly 35% of the time I will have opening bid values (12+ high-card points). And roughly half the time, I guess, I will get the chance to open the bidding. So about once in 200 hands (that doesn't sound like very often) I need to find an opening bid with a 4-4-4-1 hand.

Weak 4-4-4-1 hands are not too much of a problem playing a strong no-trump. If you have a singleton in a minor you have only one choice of bid in any event. Your worst nightmare of opening 1◇ with a singleton club and hearing partner respond 2♣ can be solved by rebidding 2NT – partner needs to check up on four-card majors if he has one because you could easily be 4-3-4-2 or 3-4-4-2 for such an auction. Hopefully it won't matter too much that you have a singleton in his first suit. When you have a singleton major it depends on what you intend to rebid. If, like me, you do not mind too much rebidding 1NT with a singleton in partner's suit, then you will open your better four-card minor, as usual. If, however, you are not prepared to rebid 1NT, then you are going to have to bid two suits, so you must open 1◇, intending to rebid 2♣.

The real problems come when you are in the 15–17 range. What I am about to suggest may sound very controversial, but I am sure is the best solution: *give serious consideration to opening 1NT despite your singleton.* Let me make my case to you:

- If you open 1NT, partner will be on firm ground. He will know how to investigate for an eight-card major-suit fit, and failing that bid 3NT. Only in extreme circumstances will he look for a minor-suit fit.
- Contrast that with the alternative. You will open one suit and then bid another. Partner will expect you to have five cards in your first suit. He may not expect you to have lots of stoppers in the third suit. He will have trouble in imagining that you are in the 15–17 range.
- When your singleton is a minor there is very little danger of your coming unstuck because partner will rarely try to play in that suit.
- The biggest danger is when your singleton is in a major and partner makes a weakness take-out into that suit and you are left to play in an unsavoury 5-1 fit. That is a real danger, I agree, sufficiently so that I only open 4-4-4-1 hands with a singleton major when the singleton is an honour card.

Easy Guide to Five-Card Majors

How should the bidding go on the following pairs of hands? If there are any alternative routes, give more than one auction

(1)
♠ A Q J 8　　♠ K 9 7
♡ K　　♡ Q 9 7 6 3
◊ K J 9 4　　◊ Q 7 5
♣ J 10 8 6　　♣ A Q

(2)
♠ A　　♠ 10 8 7 5 4 3
♡ A K J 3　　♡ Q 9 7
◊ 10 8 7 3　　◊ J 9
♣ K Q 6 2　　♣ J 7

(3)
♠ A Q 7 3　　♠ 5 2
♡ J 7 4 3　　♡ K Q
◊ 8　　◊ A Q J 3
♣ A K Q 2　　♣ J 10 9 6 3

(4)
♠ K　　♠ A J 10 7 4 3
♡ A K Q 10　　♡ 3
◊ Q 8 5 2　　◊ K 7 4
♣ 9 7 6 3　　♣ K Q 10

(5)
♠ Q　　♠ A 9 7 5 2
♡ A Q 6 3　　♡ K 7 5 4
◊ J 7 6 5　　◊ K 10 4
♣ A K 8 7　　♣ 6

(6)
♠ K Q J 3　　♠ 8 6
♡ A J 10 9　　♡ K Q 8 7
◊ Q 8 7 4　　◊ K 6
♣ K　　♣ A Q 6 3 2

(7)
♠ A Q J 4　　♠ K 5 2
♡ J　　♡ Q 10 9 5 2
◊ A J 6 4　　◊ K 7
♣ K 9 5 3　　♣ 6 4 2

(1)

♠ A Q J 8
♡ K
◊ K J 9 4
♣ J 10 8 6

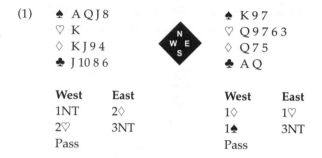

♠ K 9 7
♡ Q 9 7 6 3
◊ Q 7 5
♣ A Q

West	East
1NT	2◊
2♡	3NT
Pass	

West	East
1◊	1♡
1♠	3NT
Pass	

Nothing contentious here. Both auctions lead to the top spot without problem. It is possible that East on the second auction might prefer 2♣, fourth-suit forcing, at his second turn, but then West would rebid 3NT and there would be no reason for East to proceed.

(2)

♠ A
♡ A K J 3
◊ 10 8 7 3
♣ K Q 6 2

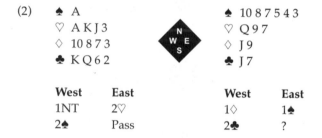

♠ 10 8 7 5 4 3
♡ Q 9 7
◊ J 9
♣ J 7

West	East
1NT	2♡
2♠	Pass

West	East
1◊	1♠
2♣	?

The best spot for East-West here is 1NT but it is hard to see a way to get there playing any methods. At least the 1NT auction ends up in 2♠ which might make but is perhaps more likely to go one down. It is hard to predict what might happen in the second auction. Would East rebid 2♠ or give simple preference to 2◊? And in either case would West pass? Most routes would end up with West in 2NT which is also likely to go one down.

(3)

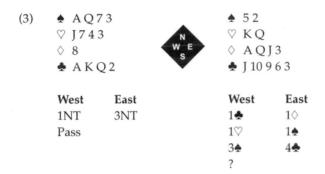

♠ A Q 7 3
♡ J 7 4 3
◇ 8
♣ A K Q 2

♠ 5 2
♡ K Q
◇ A Q J 3
♣ J 10 9 6 3

West	East
1NT	3NT
Pass	

West	East
1♣	1◇
1♡	1♠
3♣	4♣
?	

6♣ is a fair contract for East-West. On a non-trump lead, declarer's best line is to knock out the ace of hearts, intending to discard a spade on the jack of hearts and then cross-ruff. That will make whenever hearts are 4-3 and still has some chances when they are 5-2 but North is short. North will ruff the jack of hearts, East overruff and still has the spade finesse in reserve. On a trump lead, an extra trick has to be generated from somewhere. The 1NT opening has no chance of reaching the slam, while the second auction is still going strong. Some good decisions will need to be made by both players, but the slam should be bid.

(4)

♠ K
♡ A K Q 10
◇ Q 8 5 2
♣ 9 7 6 3

♠ A J 10 7 4 3
♡ 3
◇ K 7 4
♣ K Q 10

West	East
1◇	1♠
1NT	4♠
Pass	

West	East
1◇	1♠
2♣	2♡
3♡	3♠
4♠	Pass

Both auctions arrive at the top spot here, although there is not a lot to choose between 3NT and 4♠. Note, though, that the no-trump auction has given away much less information which always makes it harder for the defenders.

(5)

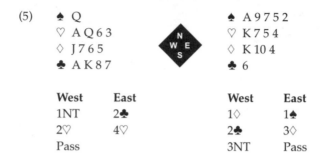

	♠ Q		♠ A 9 7 5 2
	♡ A Q 6 3		♡ K 7 5 4
	◇ J 7 6 5		◇ K 10 4
	♣ A K 8 7		♣ 6

West	East		West	East
1NT	2♣		1◇	1♠
2♡	4♡		2♣	3◇
Pass			3NT	Pass

Here the 1NT opening made it easy. Whatever East-West's methods the heart fit would be found easily enough and the best game bid. The second auction did not even find the heart fit and that is often going to be the case when responder has five spades and four hearts.

(6)

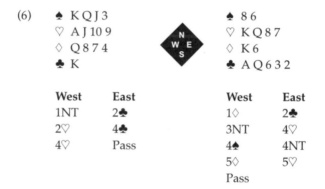

	♠ K Q J 3		♠ 8 6
	♡ A J 10 9		♡ K Q 8 7
	◇ Q 8 7 4		◇ K 6
	♣ K		♣ A Q 6 3 2

West	East		West	East
1NT	2♣		1◇	2♣
2♡	4♣		3NT	4♡
4♡	Pass		4♠	4NT
			5◇	5♡
			Pass	

Maybe the second auction has managed to survive here but it makes me feel a little ill. The first auction is straightforward, but depends on methods. East discovers the heart fit and then makes a slam try. West signs off with no diamond control and no ace of spades. If West does not open 1NT here I am not sure what he is supposed to rebid when East bids 2♣. 2NT would show 12–14 and 3NT 18–19, so I guess he goes for one or the other, in general favouring the overbid of the second auction. We are at the four level and the fit has not yet been found. East's 4♡ should be forcing (West has shown 18 points and East 12 – with less he would have bid 1♡ on the first round) and no doubt West's cue-bid confirms the fit. RKCB reveals the shortage of aces just in time.

(7)   ♠ A Q J 4   ♠ K 5 2
      ♡ J   ♡ Q 10 9 5 2
      ◇ A J 6 4   ◇ K 7
      ♣ K 9 5 3   ♣ 6 4 2

West	East		West	East
1NT	2◇		1◇	1♡
2♡	2NT		1♠	2◇
Pass			?	

The 1NT auction ends up in the reasonable 2NT, though even if East passes 2♡ the 5-1 fit would not be too bad. The second auction is harder. East has a tricky choice on the second round with no club stopper. He is a little good to pass 1♠, so gives simple preference to what will usually be a five-card suit. The spotlight now falls on West who doesn't really have quite enough to keep on bidding when East could easily have fewer values and more diamonds. If West does bid on with 2NT, surely the poor game will be reached.

WHAT HAVE WE LEARNED

A   4-4-4-1 hands are difficult, particularly when they are in your no-trump range.

B   The best thing about 4-4-4-1 hands is that they do not occur very often, so it is best not to get too worried about them.

C   Opening 1NT with a singleton in a minor or a singleton honour in a major will usually make the auction much easier, but will not necessarily lead to a better contract all of the time.

Bidding after Intervention

General Philosophy

This is the hard part. Those who play strong no-trump and four-card majors are better placed because they have already bid their major suit. Those who play weak no-trump will have benefited from its pre-emptive effect by keeping the opposition out a lot of the time, though the rest of the time they may not be able to compete part-scores effectively.

As in all competitive bidding situations the general idea is to bid your hand in as straightforward a fashion as possible. If you have a balanced hand with stopper(s) in their suit, bid no-trumps. If you have the strength and distribution to merit a forcing bid in a new suit, then do so. If you wish to bring unbid majors into the game, then make a negative double.

Negative Doubles

There are some subtle differences in negative doubles because the minor opened may not be a four-card suit. There are hands on which playing Acol you would happily make a simple or jump raise of partner's minor but feel more reluctant when the minor may be a three-card suit.

Whether or not a negative double promises four cards in any unbid majors is a constant source of argument. In my view, it depends on the level of the auction. It is perhaps acceptable to bid a four-card major at the one level, just as you would without intervention. However, when considering responding in a new suit in a competitive auction there seems to be an unalienable truth: *you should not respond in a major at the two or three level on fewer than five cards.* Having said that, it is desirable where possible for negative doubles to deliver some guarantees about unbid suits. So, we can draw up these rules:

- 1♣ – 1◊ – Double *does* promise four cards in both majors; with only one major bid it.
- 1♣ – 1♡ – Double *does* promise four spades; to bid 1♠ shows five. (This is a matter of partnership agreement; some people like to play that to bid 1♠ guarantees only a four-card suit, while to double denies four and promises both minors.)
- 1♣ – 1♠ – Double *does* promise four hearts.

- 1♣ – 2♡/2♠ – Double *does not quite* promise four cards in the other major, but will usually hold them.
- 1♣ – 2◊ – Double or 1◊ – 2♣ – Double *does not* promise four cards in both unbid majors, for it leaves a hand with, say, a 4-3-3-3 distribution and perhaps opening values no bid at all. However, having said that, partner is quite likely to respond in the major you do not have and you must be able to cope with that. So, you should either be 4-3 in the majors so at worst you are passing him out in a 4-3 fit, or you should have a stopper in the opponent's suit so you can rebid no-trumps.
- The higher the intervention becomes, the fewer guarantees in terms of distribution the double delivers. However, when opener is deciding how to respond he should always assume the doubler has four cards in any unbid majors. If the doubler does not, then that is his problem.

The values needed for a negative double depend on the level of the intervention.

- If the intervention is at the one level, about 7 points are needed because partner may rebid 1NT with 12–14. Opener should generally rebid 1NT if he does not hold four cards in any major the doubler has promised. If the overcall has not been raised it is unlikely that the doubler is short in the suit. Even if the hands contain no stopper, 1NT may still be a reasonable part-score. This is significantly preferable to rebidding 2♣, for example, on a four-card suit.
- If the intervention is at the two level, about 10–11 points are needed because partner may rebid 2NT with 12–14.
- If the intervention is at the three level, 12+ points are needed because partner may rebid 3NT with 12–14. In fact, such a double should be deemed to be game forcing, relieving opener of the need, with extra values, to jump into a suit that the doubler may not hold.

Let's look at some examples:

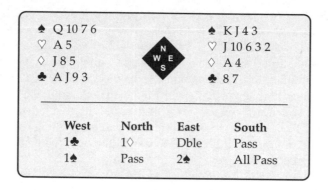

West	North	East	South
1♣	1◇	Dble	Pass
1♠	Pass	2♣	All Pass

If East had a stronger hand with game values he would bid his hand naturally by starting with his five-card suit and then bidding his four-card suit. However, this hand has no real game interest so he starts with a double. His raise when the fit has been found is made more to make it difficult for the opponents to compete than in any real hopes of game. It is known as a courtesy raise.

Note that even if South had raised to 2◇ West would have been able to introduce his spade suit, knowing that East held at least 7 or 8 points with four spades.

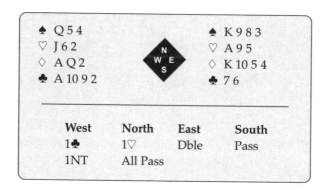

West	North	East	South
1♣	1♡	Dble	Pass
1NT	All Pass		

East's double promises four spades. Although West does not have a heart stopper, it is likely that East has heart length because South has not raised the suit. Even if East-West have no heart stopper between them they may well have seven or eight tricks once North-South have cashed their hearts.

Easy Guide to Five-Card Majors

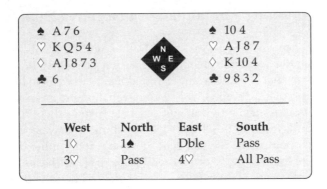

	♠ A 7 6			♠ 10 4
	♡ K Q 5 4			♡ A J 8 7
	◊ A J 8 7 3			◊ K 10 4
	♣ 6			♣ 9 8 3 2

West	North	East	South
1◊	1♠	Dble	Pass
3♡	Pass	4♡	All Pass

East's double promises four hearts. West would bid a simple 2♡ with a 4-4-3-2 distribution and a 12-count so must bid more with such a shapely 14-count. Although East is minimum, he rightly upvalues his hand because of his useful diamond holding facing West's probable five-card suit.

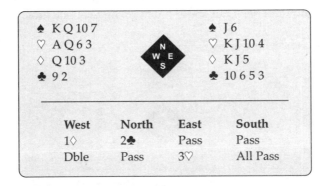

	♠ K Q 10 7			♠ J 6
	♡ A Q 6 3			♡ K J 10 4
	◊ Q 10 3			◊ K J 5
	♣ 9 2			♣ 10 6 5 3

West	North	East	South
1◊	2♣	Pass	Pass
Dble	Pass	3♡	All Pass

Although East has good values he does not have a bid over North's 2♣. He has to pass and hope that West can find a re-opening double. When West does double, East has something of a problem. At match-points it is probably best to bid a simple 2♡ because West may be very minimum to reopen when he has club shortage. However, at teams scoring East may be tempted to do more. After all, if West had a 4-4-4-1 distribution with the same 13-count that he actually holds game would be excellent.

The Continuing Auction after a Negative Double

- What it means when responder doubles and then bids a new suit is a matter of some debate. There is a school of thought that suggests that it shows a single-suited hand too weak to have bid in the first place. Personally, I have never thought this a very good idea because if the opponents compete further there may not be room to describe this hand. I don't think that weak one-suited hands should start with a negative double at all; either bid the suit despite the weakness, or pass and hope to show the suit later. For a double opener will expect a more balanced hand with all-round values. The exact meaning of a double followed by a bid in a new suit depends a little on the suits involved, but in my view it should usually show the two suits originally suggested by the double and fair values. We will look at some specific examples later on.
- A double followed by a cue-bid is generally a request for a stopper with game-forcing values.
- A double by opener, if the overcaller's partner has raised, is for take-out and need not show much in the way of extras.

Here are some examples:

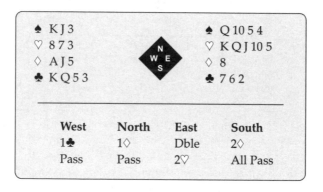

West	North	East	South
1♣	1◇	Dble	2◇
Pass	Pass	2♡	All Pass

East's initial double shows at least 4-4 in the majors. When he bids 2♡ on the next round he shows five decent hearts along with four spades. If he had invitational values or more he would have bid his hand naturally, starting with 1♡. West has virtually denied a four-card major when he passes 2◇.

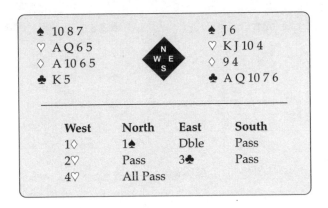

West	North	East	South
1◇	1♠	Dble	Pass
2♡	Pass	3♣	Pass
4♡	All Pass		

Here East's double guaranteed four hearts and his 3♣ rebid does not counteract that promise. So here it must be a value-showing game try. With all his values working West is happy to bid the game.

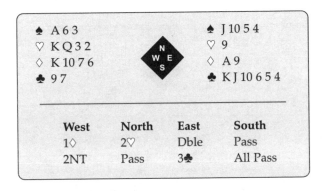

West	North	East	South
1◇	2♡	Dble	Pass
2NT	Pass	3♣	All Pass

East's sequence on this deal shows at least five good clubs and a four-card spade suit, though West has surely denied four spades. The auction shows fair values so West is allowed to bid 3NT with a club fit and a maximum hand. Here with a minimum and the worst possible club holding he is not tempted.

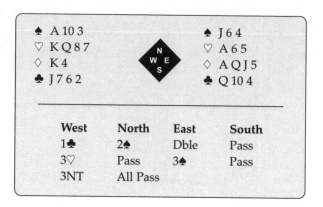

	♠ A 10 3		♠ J 6 4
	♡ K Q 8 7		♡ A 6 5
	◇ K 4		◇ A Q J 5
	♣ J 7 6 2		♣ Q 10 4

West	North	East	South
1♣	2♠	Dble	Pass
3♡	Pass	3♠	Pass
3NT	All Pass		

East's double of 2♠ will usually but not always deliver four hearts. Here if West had bid 4♡, East would have passed and hoped for the best. As it is West bid only 3♡ and East continued with a cue-bid of 3♠, asking for a stopper, and the best game was reached.

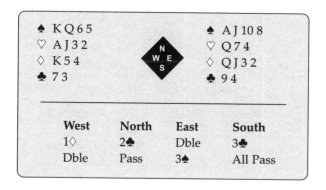

	♠ K Q 6 5		♠ A J 10 8
	♡ A J 3 2		♡ Q 7 4
	◇ K 5 4		◇ Q J 3 2
	♣ 7 3		♣ 9 4

West	North	East	South
1◇	2♣	Dble	3♣
Dble	Pass	3♠	All Pass

East doubles 2♣ because he is prepared to let West play in a 4-3 heart fit if necessary. When South raises to 3♣, West feels sure his partner must have at least one four-card major so doubles to ask him to bid it. Although West has only a balanced 13-count he knows his partner has 10 or 11 and that there must be a 4-4 fit. This is reason enough to bid. If West were to pass East would surely bid 3◇ and now West would not know what to do; either passing or bidding 3♡ would risk playing in a 4-3 fit.

Raising Partner's Minor

To my mind it is perfectly acceptable to make a simple raise of partner's minor on four-card support if there is no good alternative. However, I would prefer to bid 1NT with a balanced hand with a stopper, or double with the right holdings in any unbid suits.

However, a jump raise is another matter. While it might be reasonable to risk a jump raise of a 1♢ opener on a four-card suit because partner usually holds four diamonds, a jump raise of a 1♣ opener really should hold five trumps. Just like when a major is opened, this bid should be semi-pre-emptive, say 6–9 points.

A Cue-bid of the Suit Overcalled

A cue-bid of the suit overcalled shows a good raise to three of the minor opened. It is forcing to 2NT or three of the minor. Opener with a minimum and a stopper bids 2NT, with a maximum and a stopper bids 3NT, and without a stopper rebid the minor

No Four-card Major, No Fit, What Do I Bid?

If you have a balanced hand with no fit for opener that does not have four cards in an unbid major, you may just have to bid a four-card minor. Sequences such as 1♣ – (1♡) – 2♢ and 1♢ – (1♠) – 2♣ occasionally have to be made on four-card suits. Partner will generally rebid no-trumps when he has a balanced hand with a stopper in the suit overcalled, and if he doesn't you can cue-bid their suit on the next round to ask for half a stopper.

A Jump Cue-bid of the Suit Overcalled

Some pairs play a jump cue-bid of the suit overcalled as a stopper ask, while others prefer it to be a splinter bid. What I like, and would recommend, is for it to be a transfer to 3NT. It promises a stopper in the suit overcalled and asks opener to bid 3NT. This means you can get 3NT played from the right side when opener has Q-x or J-x-x. It also means that you have bid your hand in one bid – always a good thing to do once the auction gets competitive – and it is difficult for the opponents to get in your way.

The Opponents Double the Minor-suit Opening

When the opponents double the minor-suit opening, the emphasis changes. The auction has become competitive but neither side has yet bid any suits. If responder can describe his hand with one bid there is much more reason for him to do so. With a balanced hand it often works best to respond 1NT even with a poorish four-card major. Even if you have a 4-4 fit in that major it may break badly, or by bidding it you may make it easier for the opponents to find their fit. So if you open 1♣ or 1◇ and partner responds in a major after a take-out double, you should be more prepared to raise him with only three-card support, certainly if you have a low doubleton and maybe even with any doubleton and a trump honour.

- After a take-out double of a minor-suit opening it makes sense to play all jumps in new suits as weak, roughly the values you would need for a weak two opening at the vulnerability. (Many pairs like to play jumps as weak after any intervention over a prepared minor.)
- Note that a passed hand that jumps the bidding after any one-level suit opening should always be showing a fit for opener. He is unlikely to want to make a weak jump as he has not opened a weak two bid.
- A 2NT response after a take-out double should be natural with a fit for the minor opened. It shows about 11 points so opener can pass, raise or rebid his minor as he sees fit.
- If the opponents try to pass you out in one of your minor doubled, then believe them. I have taken a penalty from a one-level take-out double only three times that I can remember and the smallest penalty I collected was 1100. If the bidding goes 1♣ – Double – Pass – Pass, remove yourself, almost whatever your hand. Similarly, if it goes 1♣ – Pass – Pass – Double – Pass – Pass, bid something; it will almost certainly be a disaster for partner to play in 1♣.

QUIZ: BIDDING AFTER INTERVENTION

Partner opens 1♣ and the next hand overcalls 1♠. What do you bid?

(1)	(2)	(3)
♠ A Q 10	♠ 7 6	♠ J 5 4
♡ K 5 4 2	♡ A 8 7	♡ A Q 3
◊ J 10 3	◊ 9 8 4 3	◊ K J 10 5
♣ 8 7 3	♣ K J 10 4	♣ A 6 5

Partner opens 1◊ and the next hand overcalls 2♣. What do you bid?

(4)	(5)	(6)
♠ 7 2	♠ A K 7 6 3	♠ K J 5
♡ A 6 5 3	♡ A Q 3 2	♡ Q 5 2
◊ Q 9 8 4 3	◊ 8	◊ K Q 4 3
♣ 9 3	♣ J 7 6	♣ A 10 2

Partner opens 1♣ and the next hand overcalls 1♡. What do you bid?

(7)	(8)	(9)
♠ Q 10 3 2	♠ 7 6 3 2	♠ A 4 3
♡ 10 3 2	♡ A Q 10	♡ 5 4
◊ A Q 2	◊ K 10 4	◊ Q 3 2
♣ J 10 3	♣ J 7 6	♣ K J 10 5 4

Partner opens 1♣ and the next hand doubles. What do you bid?

(10)	(11)	(12)
♠ J 8 7 4	♠ K J 10 6 5 2	♠ Q 3 2
♡ A 10 2	♡ K 4	♡ Q 2
◊ Q 7 6	◊ 6 5 2	◊ A 5 4
♣ Q 10 7	♣ 8 3	♣ K 10 6 5 2

Partner opens 1◊ and the next hand doubles. What do you bid?

(13)	(14)	(15)
♠ K J 10 4 3	♠ A 3	♠ 6 5
♡ A Q 10 2	♡ 8 7	♡ A K 7 6
◊ 6 5	◊ Q 10 9 7 5	◊ 3 2
♣ Q 10	♣ J 8 7 3	♣ A K 9 8 3

Partner opens 1♣ and the next hand overcalls 1♠. What do you bid?

(1)	(2)	(3)
♠ A Q 10	♠ 7 6	♠ J 5 4
♡ K 5 4 2	♡ A 8 7	♡ A Q 3
◊ J 10 3	◊ 9 8 4 3	◊ K J 10 5
♣ 8 7 3	♣ K J 10 4	♣ A 6 5

(1)   Bid 1NT. If you double and partner has a small doubleton in spades he may be tempted to rebid a four-card minor which would not be good news. It could easily be better to play in 1NT here even if you do have a 4-4 heart fit.

(2)   Bid 2♣. A natural raise of partner's suit. Even if he has only a three-card suit it should not play too badly.

(3)   Bid 2◊. If partner bids 2NT raise him to 3NT; if he doesn't you can bid 3♠, asking him to bid 3NT with half a stopper.

Partner opens 1◊ and the next hand overcalls 2♣. What do you bid?

(4)	(5)	(6)
♠ 7 2	♠ A K 7 6 3	♠ K J 5
♡ A 6 5 3	♡ A Q 3 2	♡ Q 5 2
◊ Q 9 8 4 3	◊ 8	◊ K Q 4 3
♣ 9 3	♣ J 7 6	♣ A 10 2

(4)   Bid a simple 2◊. If you double, partner would probably bid 2♠ and you would have to correct to 3◊ which would overstate your hand.

(5)   Bid 2♠. With enough to force to game you should bid your suits naturally.

(6)   Bid 3NT. There's unlikely to be much advantage in partner being declarer, so just bid what you hope you can make.

Partner opens 1♣ and the next hand overcalls 1♡. What do you bid?

(7)	(8)	(9)
♠ Q 10 3 2	♠ 7 6 3 2	♠ A 4 3
♡ 10 3 2	♡ A Q 10	♡ 5 4
◇ A Q 2	◇ K 10 4	◇ Q 3 2
♣ J 10 3	♣ J 7 6	♣ K J 10 5 4

(7) Double. Showing four spades.

(8) Bid 1NT. It is true that a double shows four spades, which is what you have, but your heart holding suggests that partner may well not have anything in hearts and may be reluctant to bid no-trumps over a double. You do not want to risk partner bidding a three-card spade suit or a four-card minor. Even if you have a 4-4 spade fit this hand could well play better in no-trumps.

(9) Bid 2♡, showing a limit raise in clubs. Leave the rest to partner.

Partner opens 1♣ and the next hand doubles. What do you bid?

(10)	(11)	(12)
♠ J 8 7 4	♠ K J 10 6 5 2	♠ Q 3 2
♡ A 10 2	♡ K 4	♡ Q 2
◇ Q 7 6	◇ 6 5 2	◇ A 5 4
♣ Q 10 7	♣ 8 3	♣ K 10 6 5 2

(10) Bid 1NT. Once the next hand has doubled you shouldn't bid a poor four-card major with a balanced hand. It is much better to tell partner about the general nature and strength of your hand.

(11) Bid 2♠, weak. This will leave partner well placed to decide whether or not to compete if the next hand joins in.

(12) Bid 2NT. Natural with a club fit.

Partner opens 1◊ and the next hand doubles. What do you bid?

(13)	(14)	(15)
♠ K J 10 4 3	♠ A 3	♠ 6 5
♡ A Q 10 2	♡ 8 7	♡ A K 7 6
◊ 6 5	◊ Q 10 9 7 5	◊ 3 2
♣ Q 10	♣ J 8 7 3	♣ A K 9 8 3

(13) Redouble. Maybe you can take a good penalty out of the opponents in either 1♡ or 1♠. If they remove themselves to 2♣ and partner does not double you can bid 2♠ then. When you have the spade suit you are in control.

(14) Bid 3◊. This is pre-emptive just like a jump major-suit raise. However, because there is a real possibility that partner's distribution is 4-4-3-2 you should always have five trumps.

(15) Bid 2♣. When you have the values for game and you do not have spades you should always bid naturally. If you start with a redouble and the opponents pre-empt in spades you could have difficulty describing your hand.

Choose your next bid in the given auction on the hands below.

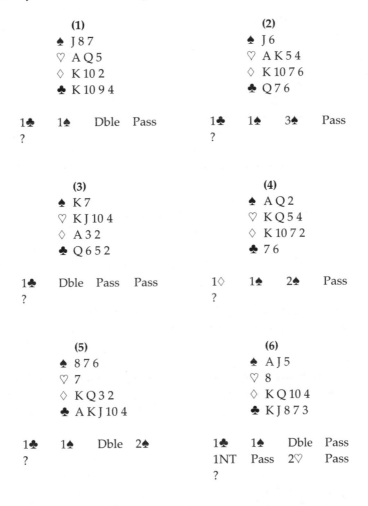

(1)

♠ J 8 7
♡ A Q 5
◇ K 10 2
♣ K 10 9 4

1♣	1♠	Dble	Pass
?			

(2)

♠ J 6
♡ A K 5 4
◇ K 10 7 6
♣ Q 7 6

1♣	1♠	3♠	Pass
?			

(3)

♠ K 7
♡ K J 10 4
◇ A 3 2
♣ Q 6 5 2

1♣	Dble	Pass	Pass
?			

(4)

♠ A Q 2
♡ K Q 5 4
◇ K 10 7 2
♣ 7 6

1◇	1♠	2♠	Pass
?			

(5)

♠ 8 7 6
♡ 7
◇ K Q 3 2
♣ A K J 10 4

1♣	1♠	Dble	2♠
?			

(6)

♠ A J 5
♡ 8
◇ K Q 10 4
♣ K J 8 7 3

1♣	1♠	Dble	Pass
1NT	Pass	2♡	Pass
?			

Choose your next bid in the given auction on the hands below.

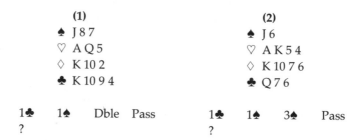

(1)
- ♠ J 8 7
- ♡ A Q 5
- ◇ K 10 2
- ♣ K 10 9 4

1♣	1♠	Dble	Pass
?			

(2)
- ♠ J 6
- ♡ A K 5 4
- ◇ K 10 7 6
- ♣ Q 7 6

1♣	1♠	3♠	Pass
?			

(1) Bid 1NT. Don't worry about not having a spade stopper. 1NT is a much better description of your hand than the alternative of rebidding 2♣ which could lead to a really silly contract. Given that the overcall was only 1♠ and it has not been raised, there is a strong likelihood that partner has something in the suit. Even if you do not have a spade stopper between your two hands, you may still have seven or eight tricks after the opponents have taken the first five.

(2) Bid 3NT. Partner's jump to 3♠ asks you to bid 3NT unless you have a really unusual hand. Partner has shown a spade stopper but would prefer you to be declarer. He probably has A-x-x or K-x-x in spades. With you as declarer the opening lead may be a low spade away from the two top honours and you will have a second stopper in the suit.

(3)
- ♠ K 7
- ♡ K J 10 4
- ◇ A 3 2
- ♣ Q 6 5 2

1♣	Dble	Pass	Pass
?			

(4)
- ♠ A Q 2
- ♡ K Q 5 4
- ◇ K 10 7 2
- ♣ 7 6

1◇	1♠	2♠	Pass
?			

(3)   Bid 1♡. If your right-hand opponent wants to defend 1♣ doubled, he is probably right. If it is a good thing for him to do, then it is bad for you. Bid your chunky four-card heart suit. If partner doesn't like hearts he can bid 1♠ or even 1NT.

(4)   Bid 3NT. 2♠ showed invitational values and a diamond fit. With 14 points and a double spade stopper you should jump to 3NT.

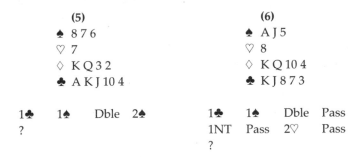

	(5)		
♠	8 7 6		
♡	7		
◇	K Q 3 2		
♣	A K J 10 4		

1♣	1♠	Dble	2♠
?			

	(6)		
♠	A J 5		
♡	8		
◇	K Q 10 4		
♣	K J 8 7 3		

1♣	1♠	Dble	Pass
1NT	Pass	2♡	Pass
?			

(5)   Double. Your double is also for take-out. Partner has promised four hearts; if you had four hearts too you would bid the suit so you must be asking partner to bid a minor. He will know your clubs are better because that is the suit you opened. Partner almost certainly has a doubleton spade on this auction, and if he has only four hearts then he must have a four-card minor so there should be a good part-score for your side.

(6)   2NT. You had a difficult decision on your first round, just as you would have done had partner responded 1♡. 1NT seemed preferable to guessing which minor to bid, but now partner has taken you out into what is probably a five-card heart suit. It would not be a good idea to pass that with a singleton. When you bid 2NT you imply a singleton heart so partner will know you have length in the minors. If he has a four-card minor he will bid it.

WHAT HAVE WE LEARNED?

A A negative double of a 1◊, 1♡ or 1♠ overcall promises at least four cards in any unbid major.

B Other negative doubles strongly suggest four cards in unbid majors but do not promise them.

C A negative double shows a minimum of about 7 or 8 points at the one level, 10 or 11 at the two level and is forcing to game if made at the three level. This is because partner may have to rebid no-trumps at that level with a balanced 12–14 points.

D If responder doubles and bids again this shows fair values and offers a choice of places to play. *It does not show a weak hand with a long suit.*

E A simple raise of the minor opened is natural and shows at least four-card support. A jump raise is semi pre-emptive (6–9) and will always have five-card support if 1♣ has been opened, but may have only four-card support for diamonds.

F A cue-bid at the two level shows at least invitational values with a four-card fit for opener. A jump cue-bid at the three level shows a stopper and asks partner to bid 3NT on any normal hand.

G A double by opener after the overcall has been raised is for take-out, denying four cards in any suit the negative doubler has promised. It does not necessarily show extra values.

H After a take-out double responder should not bother bidding a poor four-card major. If he does bid a major, opener should be more prepared to raise with three-card support.

I If the opponents think it is right to defend one of a minor doubled, believe them!

WHAT WENT WRONG?

Here is another set of 'What Went Wrong' questions to test your understanding of the material in this section. Again, I will present you with a number of deals where the bidding sequence did not arrive in the optimum contract. It is up to you to study these sequences and decide how to apportion the blame.

(1)
♠ —	♠ 7 6 3 2
♡ J 5 3	♡ 7 2
◇ K Q 10 4	◇ 8 5 2
♣ A J 9 7 6 3	♣ K Q 10 5

West	North	East	South
1♣	1♠	Pass	4♠
All Pass			

(2)
♠ Q J 10 4	♠ K 9 8 2
♡ K 7 2	♡ Q J 8 3
◇ J 10 3	◇ 7 4
♣ K Q 4	♣ J 6 2

West	North	East	South
1♣	1◇	Dble	2◇
All Pass			

(3)
♠ 9 8 4	♠ A K 6 2
♡ A Q 3	♡ 10 4
◇ K 10	◇ Q J 4 2
♣ K Q 10 7 2	♣ A J 3

West	North	East	South
1♣	2♡	Dble	Pass
3NT	Pass	6NT	All Pass

(1)
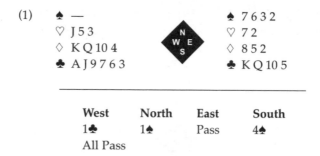

	♠ —		♠ 7 6 3 2
	♡ J 5 3		♡ 7 2
	◊ K Q 10 4		◊ 8 5 2
	♣ A J 9 7 6 3		♣ K Q 10 5

West	North	East	South
1♣	1♠	Pass	4♠
All Pass			

Here East-West let North-South play in 4♠ making with an overtrick when they themselves could have played in 5♣ going one down – not a good thing to do at any vulnerability.

Here the fault was with East. He should have dredged up a raise to 2♣ with his chunky four-card support. If his partner had a balanced 12-count with only three clubs he could hardly come to any harm, and bidding 2♣ was likely to help West with the defence if not the bidding.

That would have been all the encouragement West needed to press on to 5♣ at most vulnerabilities.

Correct auction:

West	North	East	South
1♣	1♠	2♣	4♠
5♣	. . .		

(2)   ♠ Q J 10 4   ♠ K 9 8 2
         ♡ K 7 2   ♡ Q J 8 3
         ◊ J 10 3   ◊ 7 4
         ♣ K Q 4   ♣ J 6 2

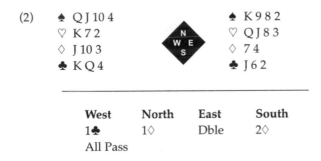

West	North	East	South
1♣	1◊	Dble	2◊
All Pass			

With East's double of 1◊ promising at least four cards in each major, West should have bid 2♠ over 2◊. Forget all notions you may have learned in the past about 'free bids' promising extra values. In today's cut-and-thrust world you have to bid when you know your side has a fit. West knows that his side has an eight-card spade fit and approximately half the points in the pack. That is sufficient information for him to want to bid 2♠.

Even non-vulnerable it would be dangerous for East to bid again since when West passes 2◊ the likelihood is that his distribution is 3-3-3-4.

Note that this auction should be a good one for strong no-trumpers. Weak no-trumpers would no doubt play in 1NT going two down while 2♠ has every chance of success.

Correct auction:

West	North	East	South
1♣	1◊	Dble	2◊
2♠	. . .		

(3)
    ♠ 9 8 4
    ♡ A Q 3
    ◊ K 10
    ♣ K Q 10 7 2

    ♠ A K 6 2
    ♡ 10 4
    ◊ Q J 4 2
    ♣ A J 3

West	North	East	South
1♣	2♡	Dble	Pass
3NT	Pass	6NT	All Pass

Playing these methods it is important to decide whether or not your hand is worth a 1NT opening at the outset, and stick to that evaluation. If you decide to upgrade it mid-auction (when you have not been asked to do so), your partner will think you are much stronger.

There would be a case for West opening 1NT in the first place, upgrading his hand on the strength of his good five-card club suit. However, having opened 1♣, when he rebid 3NT over 2♡ he showed 18–19 points, so it was perfectly reasonable for East to bid the slam.

Unfortunately, unless North decides to lead a heart, surely unlikely on the bidding, the slam has little play.

Correct auction:

West	North	East	South
1♣	2♡	Dble	Pass
2NT	Pass	3NT	All Pass

WHAT WENT WRONG?

(4)   ♠ K Q 10 4   ♠ J 6 3 2
           ♡ A 10 2   ♡ 8
           ◇ J 4 3   ◇ K Q 10 9 2
           ♣ Q 10 3   ♣ 9 8 2

West	North	East	South
1♣	Pass	1◇	Pass
1NT	Pass	2◇	All Pass

(5)   ♠ 6 5 3   ♠ 9 2
           ♡ K 4   ♡ A 9 8 2
           ◇ K 3   ◇ J 10 2
           ♣ A Q 6 5 4 3   ♣ K 10 9 2

West	North	East	South
1♣	1♠	Dble	2♠
All Pass			

(6)   ♠ J 7 6 3   ♠ K Q 10 2
           ♡ A Q J 4   ♡ 10 9 2
           ◇ Q 2   ◇ 4 3
           ♣ K 10 3   ♣ A Q J 2

West	North	East	South
		1♣	Pass
1♡	Pass	1NT	Pass
3NT	All Pass		

(4)
   ♠ K Q 10 4
   ♡ A 10 2
   ◇ J 4 3
   ♣ Q 10 3

   ♠ J 6 3 2
   ♡ 8
   ◇ K Q 10 9 2
   ♣ 9 8 2

West	North	East	South
1♣	Pass	1◇	Pass
1NT	Pass	2◇	All Pass

East was wrong here. He should have bid his four-card major before his five-card diamond suit. On this occasion that would have found the spade fit and led to a higher-scoring part-score, not particularly important at teams scoring but crucial at match-pointed pairs.

Suppose that there had not been a 4-4 spade fit and West had rebid 1NT over 1♠, can East now introduce his diamonds, or would that show five spades? This is a matter for individual partnerships to decide but my recommendation would be for the 2◇ bid to promise at least five diamonds; if East had five spades and four diamonds he would have to choose between passing 1NT and rebidding 2♠ depending on the general texture of his hand.

As it went, East-West were lucky that North-South did not get together in hearts, though they may yet do so after West passes 2◇. An initial 1♠ response and raise to 2♠ would have made heart intervention more difficult.

Correct auction:

West	North	East	South
1♣	Pass	1♠	Pass
2♠	. . .		

(5) ♠ 6 5 3 ♠ 9 2
     ♡ K 4 ♡ A 9 8 2
     ◇ K 3 ◇ J 10 2
     ♣ A Q 6 5 4 3 ♣ K 10 9 2

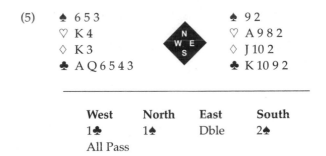

West	North	East	South
1♣	1♠	Dble	2♠
All Pass			

Here West was too conservative. Assuming that North-South have a combined eight-card fit then it is very likely that East-West have an eight-card fit too, and it is surely likely that that fit is in clubs.

When you open a prepared 1♣ but actually have a club suit, the onus is on you to tell partner so. On this deal West should bid 3♣ over 2♠ and then if North-South press on to 3♠ East should compete further with 4♣.

Correct auction:

West	North	East	South
1♣	1♠	Dble	2♠
3♣	. . .		

(6) ♠ J 7 6 3   ♠ K Q 10 2
     ♡ A Q J 4   ♡ 10 9 2
     ◇ Q 2   ◇ 4 3
     ♣ K 10 3   ♣ A Q J 2

West	North	East	South
		1♣	Pass
1♡	Pass	1NT	Pass
3NT	All Pass		

Both players might have ensured that the 4-4 spade fit was located on this deal.

Although it is normal either to open or rebid no-trumps when you have a balanced hand, East's actual distribution is an exception. By rebidding 1NT in preference to 1♠ he would have made it impossible for his side to play in spades when his partner had a weak hand. With four cards in the suit opened he should have rebid 1♠ in the first place.

However, when East actually rebid 1NT it was still possible that he held a four-card spade suit in a 4-3-3-3 hand. So West should have used Checkback. East would have rebid 2♡ and West could have bid 2♠. When East raised to 3♠ the fit would have been found and the 50% game reached.

Correct auction:

West	North	East	South
		1♣	Pass
1♡	Pass	1♠	Pass
4♠	All Pass		

(7) ♠ A K 2
 ♡ 7 3
 ◊ K Q J 10 4
 ♣ A J 2

♠ 7 6
♡ A K 9 8 2
◊ A 6 3 2
♣ 10 4

West	North	East	South
1◊	Pass	1♡	Pass
2NT	Pass	3◊	Pass
3NT	All Pass		

(8) ♠ 8 2
 ♡ A 8 2
 ◊ Q 10 9 3
 ♣ A K 8 2

♠ K Q 7 3
♡ K 4
◊ A K J 8 2
♣ 7 3

West	North	East	South
1♣	Pass	1♠	Pass
1NT	Pass	3NT	All Pass

(9) ♠ A K Q J
 ♡ 9 3 2
 ◊ Q 7 6
 ♣ J 9 6

♠ 7 2
♡ A K 10 4
◊ J 10 3
♣ Q 10 4 3

West	North	East	South
1♣	Pass	1♡	Pass
1♠	Pass	3♣	All Pass

(7) ♠ A K 2
     ♡ 7 3
     ◇ K Q J 10 4
     ♣ A J 2

♠ 7 6
♡ A K 9 8 2
◇ A 6 3 2
♣ 10 4

West	North	East	South
1◇	Pass	1♡	Pass
2NT	Pass	3◇	Pass
3NT	All Pass		

Here West failed to realise the potential of his hand. Given that 3♣ from East would have been Checkback, his actual choice of 3◇ showed genuine slam interest in diamonds. West's hand is hugely suitable for a diamond slam.

He should have bid 3♠ over 3◇ and then, when East signed off in 3NT, pressed on with 4♣. That would be all East needed to bid the slam with his excellent controls.

Correct auction:

West	North	East	South
1◇	Pass	1♡	Pass
2NT	Pass	3◇	Pass
3♠	Pass	3NT	Pass
4♣	Pass	6◇	All Pass

(8)

♠ 8 2		♠ K Q 7 3	
♡ A 8 2		♡ K 4	
◇ Q 10 9 3		◇ A K J 8 2	
♣ A K 8 2		♣ 7 3	

West	North	East	South
1♣	Pass	1♠	Pass
1NT	Pass	3NT	All Pass

Although it is right to respond in a four-card major before a five-card diamond suit on a hand with no game interest, when you have game-forcing values you should bid your suits in the right order or there is danger of missing slam, as here.

Had East responded 1◇ in the first place, West would have raised to 2◇ rather than rebid no-trumps. (Don't be fooled into rebidding no-trumps when you have four-card support for partner's 1◇ response – you should raise for most of the time he will have a five-card suit and raising diamonds will make it much easier for your side to bid your hands properly.) This would immediately alert East to the possibility of a slam which should be reached after a number of cue-bids.

Correct auction:

West	North	East	South
1♣	Pass	1◇	Pass
2◇	Pass	2♠	Pass
2NT	Pass	3♡	Pass
4♣	Pass	4◇	Pass
4♡	Pass	6◇	All Pass

(9) ♠ A K Q J   ♠ 7 2
   ♡ 9 3 2   ♡ A K 10 4
   ◇ Q 7 6   ◇ J 10 3
   ♣ J 9 6   ♣ Q 10 4 3

West	North	East	South
1♣	Pass	1♡	Pass
1♠	Pass	3♣	All Pass

Here West suffered for not showing a balanced hand when he had a balanced hand. When he rebid 1♠ over East's 1♡, East thought he had at least four clubs. As East had no diamond stopper it seemed foolish for him to bid no-trumps, so instead he showed invitational values with four-card club support. This should have led to a sensible part-score, and indeed the contract has reasonable hopes of succeeding, particularly if the defenders lead diamonds. If the opposing diamonds break 4-3 those in no-trumps are likely to make eight tricks compared with nine in clubs; if the opposing diamonds break 5-2 then there will be only seven tricks in no-trumps but 3♣ is likely to go one down.

East did not have sufficient values to bid fourth-suit forcing over 1♠ as if he later supported clubs he would have shown game-forcing values.

Correct auction:

West	North	East	South
1♣	Pass	1♡	Pass
1NT	All Pass		

PART III
CLEVER STUFF

The purpose of this section is to introduce you to some fairly simple conventions which are not necessary but may make your life easier within a strong no-trump, five-card major system. All of them are in widespread use in the five-card-major world.

Inverted Minor-suit Raises

When we open a major suit we have a plethora of ways in which to make some sort of strong raise: we can bid 3♣ or 3♢ with less than a game force; or 2NT or a splinter bid when we are stronger. When we open a minor it is not so easy: a 2NT response is natural, and we are used to playing jump-shifts as natural. Most responding hands don't give us a problem but every once in a while we have a good hand with a primary fit for partner and no good bid.

Playing inverted minor-suit raises, a simple raise of partner's minor is forcing for one round, whereas a double jump is weaker – a regular single raise but with five trumps. Where exactly you draw the line between the two is a matter for some partnership discussion. Some people also use a jump in the other minor to show a limit raise in the minor opened and this treatment allows the inverted raise to be played as game-forcing. However, that is not a treatment we will adopt in this book.

Here are some points to consider about inverted minor bidding:

- The jump raise denies a four-card major.
- If partner makes a jump raise, always pass with a balanced hand with 12–14 points, but always bid on (usually 3NT) when you have 18+. With an unbalanced hand somewhere in the middle, use your judgement, but remember the power of a 5-5 fit.
- Some people like to play that a single raise also denies a four-card major but I do not see why that is necessary. Surely with five cards in partner's minor and a four-card major on the side with at least invitational values, there can be no harm in raising immediately.

- The question of how forcing the simple raise is must be addressed. I would suggest that either three of the suit opened or 2NT can be passed in any sequence. Once the bidding has progressed beyond that level game must be reached.

Here are some example sequences:

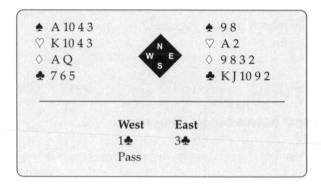

♠ A 10 4 3		♠ 9 8
♡ K 10 4 3		♡ A 2
◇ A Q		◇ 9 8 3 2
♣ 7 6 5		♣ K J 10 9 2

West	East
1♣	3♣
Pass	

Although East has a fair hand, it is nowhere near worth a game try if partner has a weak no-trump. West should pass without thought. Just because he has three small trumps and good stoppers in the other suits is no reason to bid 3NT. Although that contract may have fair play here, next time partner will be weaker.

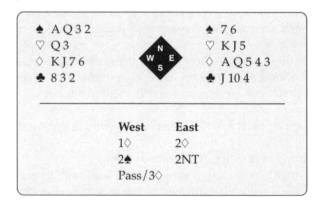

♠ A Q 3 2		♠ 7 6
♡ Q 3		♡ K J 5
◇ K J 7 6		◇ A Q 5 4 3
♣ 8 3 2		♣ J 10 4

West	East
1◇	2◇
2♠	2NT
Pass/3◇	

After the forcing single raise West bids his four-card spade suit (denying four hearts – with both he would bid hearts first), and East limits his hand with 2NT. It is close now whether West should pass or convert back to 3◇. It is also close as to which is the better contract.

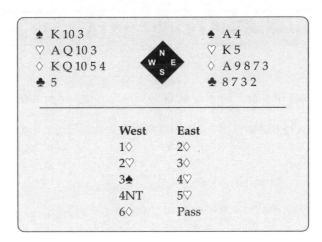

	West	East
	1◊	2◊
	2♡	3◊
	3♠	4♡
	4NT	5♡
	6◊	Pass

After West shows his second suit and East limits his hand with 3◊, West goes on with 3♠. He is likely to have his actual distribution, but could be 2-4-5-2 without a club stopper. East's hand is hugely suitable and he wants to make a forward-going move. The obvious bid is 4♠ but that will leave partner in doubt about the king of hearts. The clever thing for East to do is bid the card that West cannot find out about via RKCB. Now it cannot hurt West to use RKCB – if East has only one ace they can stop in 5◊, but when he shows up with two the good slam is reached.

QUIZ: INVERTED MINOR-SUIT RAISES

What do you bid next on the following hands with the sequences below?

(1)	(2)	(3)
♠ K J 10 4	♠ Q 4	♠ K 10 4
♡ 6	♡ K 6 5	♡ 7
◊ A Q 10 7 6	◊ K Q 10 7 6	◊ A 9 8 5
♣ A 6 4	♣ 6 3 2	♣ A J 6 5 2

(1)		(2)		(3)	
1◊	2◊	1◊	2◊	1♣	2♣
2♠	?	2♡	3◊	2◊	2NT
		3♠	?	?	

	(1)		**(2)**		**(3)**
♠	K J 10 4	♠	Q 4	♠	K 10 4
♡	6	♡	K 6 5	♡	7
◇	A Q 10 7 6	◇	K Q 10 7 6	◇	A 9 8 5
♣	A 6 4	♣	6 3 2	♣	A J 6 5 2

1◇	2◇	1◇	2◇	1♣	2♣
2♠	?	2♡	3◇	2◇	2NT
		3♠	?	?	

(1) Bid 4♡. Partner has shown four spades. Although he probably has a weak no-trump hand, he may be unbalanced or even be balanced with 18–19. You do know that he has at least four diamonds, for the only time he opens with three is when he is 4-4-3-2 and you know he does not have four hearts. 4♡ is a splinter bid agreeing spades. You show your exact distribution and leave the rest to partner; if he has no wasted values in hearts there could easily be a slam on.

Perhaps he has:

> ♠ A Q 6 5
> ♡ 8 7 2
> ◇ K 9 8 2
> ♣ K 5

when slam in either suit is excellent.

(2) Bid 5◇. This to some degree is a matter of partnership style, but in my view a jump to game in a forcing situation when the other hand is unlimited should show a minimum hand in which all the values are working. That way partner can bid a slam when he has:

> ♠ K J 6
> ♡ A 9 8 3
> ◇ A 9 8 5 4 2
> ♣ —

and pass when he has:

---

140   *Easy Guide to Five-Card Majors*

♠ A 6 2
♡ A Q J 2
◊ A 9 8 5
♣ A 4

(3) Bid 3♠. Remember that partner did not bid 2NT directly over 1♣, so is quite likely to have five-card club support. While it could certainly be right to pass 2NT – it all depends on how well the hands fit together – it is my least favourite contract. How likely is it that partner will make exactly eight tricks in no-trumps here? If you bid 3♠ you describe your distribution perfectly and partner can choose between 3NT and 5♣. Perhaps partner has:

♠ A J 2
♡ A 10 3
◊ 7 2
♣ Q 10 7 4 3

in which case 5♣ is practically laydown (you can manoeuvre to eliminate both red suits before playing ace and another club to force the opponents into opening up spades for you) while 3NT is on a finesse.

Or he may have:

♠ Q 9 2
♡ K Q 10
◊ J 2
♣ K 10 9 8 3

Where 5♣ is hopeless but 3NT depends only on guessing which opponent holds the jack of spades (provided you don't lose a club trick).

The Forcing 1NT Response and Two-over-one Game-forcing

Our system, as we have defined it, requires responder to have in the region of 11 HCP to respond at the two level. And over this response, opener will often rebid 2NT with 12–14 points. He cannot choose to bid 3NT with 14 points if he so wishes, because that rebid would show 18+. So when opener does rebid 2NT, responder has to guess whether or not to raise to 3NT when he has 11 or 12 points; and at teams scoring, most aggressive players will do so most of the time.

It is but a tiny step from here to say that the two-level response in the first place should be played as forcing to game, which can be enormously helpful in slam auctions. In addition to the sequences we discussed on page 33, the following sequences become forcing:

West	East
1♠	2♣
2♠	2NT

West	East
1♠	2♣
2♡	2NT

West	East
1♠	2♣
3♣	

The one sequence that such methods often allow to be dropped is when responder rebids his suit, e.g. 1♠ – 2♣ – 2♠ – 3♣. This means that moderate hands with very long suits do not have to risk responding 1NT on the first round.

It is unarguable that playing a two-over-one response as game-forcing makes bidding the hands that start that way easier, but of course it does mean that all weaker hands with no suit to bid at the one level must start with 1NT. And over this 1NT response, opener, even with a 5-3-3-2 distribution, must find a bid. The convention is for opener, with such a 5-3-3-2 distribution, to respond in his lower three-card suit.

While not being able to play two fairly balanced hands of limited combined values in 1NT is a distinct drawback, playing the 1NT response as forcing does give its users another tier of bidding. It is too complex a subject to go into in much detail here, but consider for a moment the following possibilities:

- A direct major-suit raise, whether simple or a jump, can have a different meaning depending on whether it is made straight away or via a forcing 1NT response.

- A bid of 2NT can have a different meaning depending on whether it is made directly or after a forcing 1NT.
- A special meaning can be assigned to a bid of 2♠ after the sequence 1♡ – 1NT – 2♣/◇/♡.
- On pages 40–2 we looked at Bergen raises and decided that it was important to be able to differentiate between a three-card raise (3♣) and a four-card raise (3◇). However, playing a forcing no-trump it would be normal to start the three-card limit raises with a 1NT response, thereby freeing the initial 3♣ response for something else – perhaps allowing 3♣ and 3◇ to show different strengths of four-card raise for example.

There are many possibilities, limited only by the imagination of the partnership.

Because there are so many different possibilities for each partnership to decide on if they are going to employ a forcing 1NT response it seems more helpful to use the quiz section to demonstrate some of the advantages of playing two-over-one as game-forcing.

QUIZ: TWO-OVER-ONE GAME-FORCING

Playing two-over-one game-forcing, how should the bidding go on the following pairs of hands?

(1)
♠ A K 6 5 2		♠ 7 3
♡ A 2	N	♡ K 6 5
◇ 6 5	W E	◇ A Q
♣ A J 6 3	S	♣ K 10 9 5 4 2

(2)
♠ K		♠ Q J 10 5 4 2
♡ Q 5 3 2	N	♡ 8
◇ K Q 10 3 2	W E	◇ A 8
♣ A J 3	S	♣ K Q 6 5

(3)
♠ A K J 6 5		♠ Q 4
♡ J 10 5 4	N	♡ K Q 3
◇ A 7 6	W E	◇ K Q 9 2
♣ 6	S	♣ A 10 4 3

(1) ♠ A K 6 5 2   ♠ 7 3
     ♡ A 2   ♡ K 6 5
     ◊ 6 5   ◊ A Q
     ♣ A J 6 3   ♣ K 10 9 5 4 2

West	East
1♠	2♣
3♣	3◊
3♡	3NT
4♣	4♡
4NT	5♠
7♣	Pass

The ability to make a forcing raise of responder's suit is enormously helpful. Without such an agreement West would have had to choose between 3NT or 4♣, both of which are space-consuming and not very descriptive. East is minimum but suitable so cue-bids his diamond values before signing off in 3NT. West now presses on, surely confirming four-card club support, and East cue-bids in hearts. West is never stopping short of a small slam now so can afford to check up on aces. Because his sixth trump is effectively as good as the queen, East responds 5♠ and West can see that the grand must have good play. If East held as little as ♠xx ♡Kxx ◊Axx ♣KQxxx it would need a 3-3 spade break but any outside queen, or the jack of hearts, or a sixth trump would make it much better.

(2) ♠ K   ♠ Q J 10 5 4 2
     ♡ Q 5 3 2   ♡ 8
     ◊ K Q 10 3 2   ◊ A 8
     ♣ A J 3   ♣ K Q 6 5

West	East
	1♠
2◊	2♠
2NT	3♣
3♠	4♠
Pass	

This type of deal is notoriously difficult for standard methods. West needs to investigate whether to play in 3NT or 4♠. Playing standard methods West would need to rebid either 3♣ or 3♡ over 2♠. If he bids 3♣ he risks being raised when 3NT is the right spot; if he bids 3♡ he risks playing 3NT facing shortage in that suit. In the two-over-one auction he is able to make a 'waiting bid' of 2NT. If East raises straight to 3NT then he will be balanced and 3NT is likely to be the best game; however, if East has some extra distributional feature he can show it. Over 3♣ West can show his limited support for spades and East is happy to choose that game.

(3)

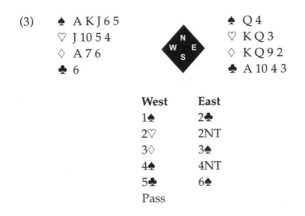

	♠ A K J 6 5		♠ Q 4
	♡ J 10 5 4		♡ K Q 3
	◇ A 7 6		◇ K Q 9 2
	♣ 6		♣ A 10 4 3

West	East
1♠	2♣
2♡	2NT
3◇	3♠
4♠	4NT
5♣	6♠
Pass	

Here East can bid a forcing 2NT over 2♡ and West continues to show his distribution. East's 3♠ shows the doubleton honour and West, with a strong spade suit himself, is happy to choose that game. West's distribution seems to fit perfectly with East's hand, so East wheels out RKCB and the three-ace response propels East-West to slam.

Flannery

Flannery is another convention that is very popular in the USA, and in truth it goes well with a forcing 1NT response and five-card majors.

You may have noticed that when I was addressing the problem of how to rebid over a forcing 1NT with a balanced hand I said that the normal agreement was to rebid your lower three-card suit. So what do you do when you are 4-5-2-2 with insufficient values to make a reverse bid? This hand-type is clearly difficult. Some players decide that if they have to rebid 2♣ on the 4-5-2-2 distribution, then they might as well rebid 2♣ whenever they have a balanced hand. At least then their 2◊ rebid becomes natural.

The other solution is to play a Flannery 2◊ opening. Playing Flannery, an opening 2◊ shows exactly five hearts and four spades with 12–15 points, i.e. not enough for a reverse bid.

Because the bid is so specific, responder is well placed simply to bid the final contract, or he can invite game by jumping to 3♡ or 3♠. Alternatively, he can bid 2NT to find out more about opener's hand. The following is a widely played structure:

2◊	2NT
3♣	shows three clubs (i.e. 4-5-1-3)
3◊	shows three diamonds (i.e. 4-5-3-1)
3♡	shows 4-5-2-2 distribution, minimum (i.e. 12–13)
3♠	shows 4-5-2-2 distribution, maximum (i.e. 14–15), with the values mostly in the major suits
3NT	shows 4-5-2-2 distribution, maximum (i.e. 14–15), with the values mostly in the minor suits
4♣	shows four clubs (i.e. 4-5-0-4)
4◊	shows four diamonds (i.e. 4-5-4-0)

Individual partnerships need to agree on the continuations, in particular which sequences are forcing and which not.

Note that if you play Flannery there is no longer any necessity to respond to 1♡ with a four-card spade suit since you know that partner cannot have four spades unless he has the values to bid again. So if a Flannery partnership have the sequence: 1♡ – 1♠ – 2♠ against you, then it is certain that the fit is 5-3. This is quite an advantage since for most pairs this is a problem area. If it is correct to respond 1♠ to a 1♡

opening with a poor four-card major just in case you have a 4-4 spade fit, should you raise with three-card support or rebid 1NT (assuming that you are in range)? If you raise, you risk playing in a very poor fit while if you rebid 1NT you risk missing a superior 5-3 fit.

Here are a couple of examples of Flannery in action:

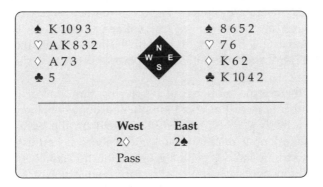

	West	East
	2◇	2♠
	Pass	

Flannery pairs keep low in 2♠ when most other pairs would bid 1♡ – 1♠ – 3♠ which may well go down.

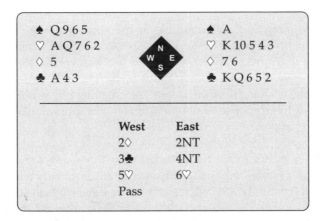

	West	East
	2◇	2NT
	3♣	4NT
	5♡	6♡
	Pass	

There may be other routes to slam here but Flannery has made it easy. Once West is known to have a singleton diamond, Blackwood answers all East's remaining problems. Whether this is straightforward Blackwood or Key Card (there can be problems knowing which major is agreed) is a matter for individual partnerships.

Support Doubles

First we had the straightforward take-out double; then the negative double, followed by various types of responsive and competitive treatments of this useful call. However, in the UK many experienced club and regular tournament players have not given much thought to the situation where an opponent overcalls in fourth position, after there has been an opening bid and a response in a new suit. On occasions when I have sat down with an unfamiliar partner to discuss system before duplicate I have mentioned this situation and received the answer: 'I don't know. Penalties, I suppose.'

In truth, there is no more sense in playing this type of double for penalties than any of the above-mentioned doubles. However, what meaning is best assigned to it does depend on the basic methods. Playing a weak no-trump and four-card majors it is best used to show a strong no-trump hand-type that is unsuitable for actually bidding no-trumps, i.e. one with no stopper or a stopper such as A-x or A-x-x. But playing five-card majors and a strong no-trump, there is much less need for this meaning since most of those hands will have been opened 1NT in the first place, and if they are too strong for that then a general unassuming cue-bid will suffice.

Playing support doubles, a double in the above-mentioned position shows three-card support for responder, freeing the direct raise to guarantee four-card support. Whether or not you choose to adopt this approach after all one-level openings is up to you, but I would certainly recommend it after prepared minor-suit openings. It is also usual to play that if the response is doubled, then a redouble similarly shows three-card support.

To what degree does a failure to double deny three cards in responder's suit? This is a matter for partnership agreement, but in my view any bid other than double should categorically deny three cards in responder's suit. A pass, on the other hand, should be allowed when very unsuitable for competing further. Although the double does not show extra values, it should be remembered that if the opponents continue to pass, the double does *force* responder to bid something. Therefore it is not sound to double on a minimum hand with poor three-card support and significant values in the suit overcalled. That is simply likely to exchange a plus score for a minus.

Here are some examples of the support double/redouble at work:

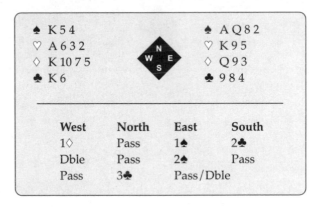

	West	North	East	South
	1◇	Pass	1♠	2♣
	Dble	Pass	2♠	Pass
	Pass	3♣	Pass/Dble	

Here if not playing support doubles West would probably have tried 2♠ which might have persuaded East to make some sort of game try. However, knowledge that he is facing only three-card support will surely persuade East to take the cautious view. And if North-South press on to 3♣ he will choose to defend, either doubled or undoubled depending on the form of scoring and his general philosophy of life.

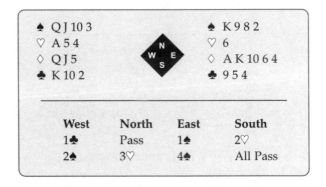

	West	North	East	South
	1♣	Pass	1♠	2♡
	2♠	3♡	4♠	All Pass

Here knowledge that his partner has four-card spade support allows East to have a pot at game once it becomes likely that West does not have too many wasted values in hearts. If three-card support was a possibility, East would have been hesitant about being so exuberant.

The double does not have to show a weak no-trump hand-type; it can be the first move on a number of stronger hands.

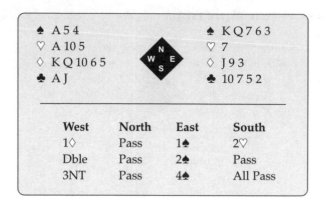

♠ A 5 4			♠ K Q 7 6 3
♡ A 10 5			♡ 7
◇ K Q 10 6 5			◇ J 9 3
♣ A J			♣ 10 7 5 2

West	North	East	South
1◇	Pass	1♠	2♡
Dble	Pass	2♠	Pass
3NT	Pass	4♠	All Pass

The support double enabled West to show three-card spade support in his strong balanced hand. East, with a decent five-card spade suit and singleton heart had an easy decision to go back to spades.

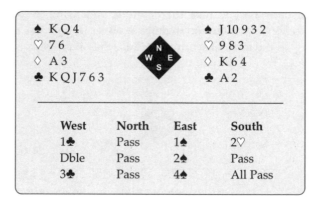

♠ K Q 4			♠ J 10 9 3 2
♡ 7 6			♡ 9 8 3
◇ A 3			◇ K 6 4
♣ K Q J 7 6 3			♣ A 2

West	North	East	South
1♣	Pass	1♠	2♡
Dble	Pass	2♠	Pass
3♣	Pass	4♠	All Pass

West doubles before bidding 3♣ to show three-card spade support and extra values (without extra values he would have passed 2♠). This makes it easy for East to bid the good but thin game.

Passed Hand Bidding

When partner is a passed hand, the player in third (and to some degree fourth) seat likes to be allowed a little more freedom when it comes to his choice of opening bid. He might like to open a five-card major on 9 or 10 high-card points, or perhaps open a chunky four-card major on occasion. He hopes that this tactic will make life more difficult for his opponents. The last thing he needs is a partner who cannot take a joke! In particular, he does not want partner to raise him to the three level or higher without very good reason.

The Americans are very fond of the Drury convention. This is a simple little gadget whereby a response by a passed hand of 2♣ to an opening 1♡/1♠ shows a near-maximum pass (say 9–11 points) and promises three- (or even four-) card support. If opener has no game interest whatsoever he rebids his major and there the matter rests (usually); otherwise he makes some other rebid which keeps game in the picture.

On the negative side, of course, is the loss of a natural 2♣ response, but there are various ways around this. A 3♣ response can be used to show 9 or 10 points and a six-card club suit. Alternatively, for those who like to play weak two openings in diamonds, hearts and spades, why not play 2♢ as Drury? Most hands that would want to respond a natural 2♢ would have already opened a weak two in the suit, whereas the same could not be said about clubs.

On the other hand, why not simply respond 1NT on most hands anyway, since that is what you would have done had you not been a passed hand? In my favourite five-card major partnerships I do not play Drury but I do have the agreement that two of a minor by a passed hand is natural(ish) but also promises three-card support for the major opened. It seems to me that I have the best of both worlds: not only can I show the support immediately, but I can also help partner decide whether or not his hand fits with mine.

Of course, none of this gets in the way of the tried and tested method of showing a maximum pass with a fit for partner – jumping in a new suit. If you reject all that has gone before in this section, then you could play that a jump in a new suit after passing is natural with three-card support (Bergen raises no longer apply), but if you have decided to adopt other ways of showing a three-card raise, then the jump in a new suit should show four-card support. A 2NT response becomes the general limit raise, so that a double jump is still pre-emptive.

WHAT HAVE WE LEARNED?

It should be stressed that all the conventions discussed in this section are optional. If you are happy with what you have learned in the first two sections, then feel free to leave all this alone.

A   A simple raise of a minor suit is forcing for at least one round with primary support. It may contain a four-card major. Any bid of 2NT or three of the minor may be passed, but all other bids below game are forcing.

B   A jump raise in a minor shows five-card support and is non-forcing. It shows about 6–9 points.

C   A two-over-one response can be played as game-forcing, making some constructive bidding easier. This needs to be allied to a forcing 1NT response.

D   The Flannery 2◊ convention goes well with a forcing 1NT response. Using this convention a 2◊ opening shows five hearts, four spades and 12–15 points.

E   If you decide to play the Flannery 2◊ then you need a five-card suit to respond 1♠ to a 1♡ opening because partner cannot have four spades unless he is going to introduce them on the second round.

F   When fourth hand intervenes after partner has responded to our prepared minor in a new suit, then a double is best played as showing three-card support for responder.

G   There are several methods in use to show a maximum pass with three-card support for opener. One commonly played convention is Drury (actually the method I have described here is technically called Reverse Drury). Playing Drury, a 2♣ response to one of a major by a passed hand shows a maximum pass with three (or four) cards in the suit opened. Opener signs off in the major with no game interest.

Study these sequences and decide how to apportion the blame. Assume that the system includes inverted minor raises, two-over-one game-forcing, forcing 1NT response, Flannery, support doubles and Drury.

(1)   ♠ Q 4 3   ♠ A J 10 2
      ♡ K Q 10 2   ♡ 9 4
      ◇ A Q 10   ◇ 7 6
      ♣ J 10 4   ♣ K Q 7 3 2

West	North	East	South
1♣	Pass	2♣	Pass
2♡	Pass	2♠	Pass
2NT	All Pass		

(2)   ♠ K   ♠ A Q 6 3 2
      ♡ A J 10 3   ♡ 7
      ◇ 9 7 2   ◇ A 10 6 3
      ♣ K Q J 8 3   ♣ A 9 2

West	North	East	South
		1♠	Pass
2♣	Pass	2◇	Pass
3NT	All Pass		

(3)   ♠ A 7 6   ♠ J 8 5 3 2
      ♡ A K 7 6 2   ♡ Q 8
      ◇ 7   ◇ K 10 3 2
      ♣ K Q J 7   ♣ 9 3

West	North	East	South
1♡	Pass	1♠	Pass
2♣	Pass	2♡	Pass
3♠	All Pass		

(1)

♠ Q 4 3			♠ A J 10 2
♡ K Q 10 2			♡ 9 4
◊ A Q 10			◊ 7 6
♣ J 10 4			♣ K Q 7 3 2

West	North	East	South
1♣	Pass	2♣	Pass
2♡	Pass	2♠	Pass
2NT	All Pass		

After an inverted minor-suit raise all bids of 2NT or three of the minor opened are non-forcing. Here, after the raise, both East and West showed their four-card suits, but then it was up to West to decide how high he wanted to play facing 10 or 11 points in the East hand. His actual choice of 2NT showed about 12 or a poor 13 points and East was quite right not to proceed, though at teams scoring he might have chosen to go back to clubs with such a pure hand as that was likely to be the safer part-score.

With a bulging 14-count including three tens West should have bid 3NT.

Correct auction:

West	North	East	South
1♣	Pass	2♣	Pass
2♡	Pass	2♠	Pass
3NT	All Pass		

ANSWERS TO WHAT WENT WRONG?

(2)

♠ K		♠ A Q 6 3 2
♡ A J 10 3		♡ 7
◊ 9 7 2		◊ A 10 6 3
♣ K Q J 8 3		♣ A 9 2

West	North	East	South
		1♠	Pass
2♣	Pass	2◊	Pass
3NT	All Pass		

West's 3NT rebid was premature in a two-over-one auction. He should simply have rebid 2NT to see if East had anything interesting to say. Here East would have shown his club support and suddenly West's hand gets better . . . and better. Cue-bidding should now lead to the excellent slam.

Standard methods are inadequate here. True, West could have chosen 2♡, fourth-suit forcing, but now when East bids 3♣ that need not be three-card support and the singleton heart is no certainty. If West then bids 3NT it suggests doubt about no-trumps, i.e. probably with only one heart stopper.

Correct auction:

West	North	East	South
		1♠	Pass
2♣	Pass	2◊	Pass
2NT	Pass	3♣	Pass
3♡	Pass	3♠	Pass
4♣	Pass	4◊	Pass
4♡	Pass	4♠	Pass
6♣	All Pass		

(3) ♠ A 7 6
     ♡ A K 7 6 2
     ◊ 7
     ♣ K Q J 7

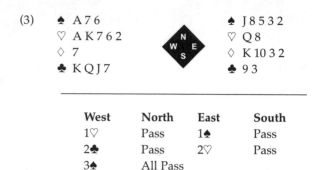

♠ J 8 5 3 2
♡ Q 8
◊ K 10 3 2
♣ 9 3

West	North	East	South
1♡	Pass	1♠	Pass
2♣	Pass	2♡	Pass
3♠	All Pass		

Although 3♠ will make most of the time, sometimes trumps will break 4-1 and it will go down.

Here it was completely unnecessary for East-West to get that high. If West had had a minimum hand he would have raised East's 1♠ to 2♠ on the first round; 1♠ showed five spades, remember. When West first introduced his club suit and then showed his three-card spade support he was showing significant extra values, i.e. about 15–17 high-card points. There was no need for him to jump the bidding.

Correct auction:

West	North	East	South
1♡	Pass	1♠	Pass
2♣	Pass	2♡	Pass
2♠	All Pass		

(4)
♠ 8 7 3
♡ K J 10 6
♢ K 2
♣ K Q J 4

♠ K Q 5 4 2
♡ 8
♢ Q J 10 5
♣ A 10 3

West	North	East	South
1♣	Pass	1♠	2♡
Dble	Pass	4♠	All Pass

(5)
♠ K 10 9 4 3
♡ Q 10 5 4
♢ K 2
♣ K 4

♠ Q J 7
♡ A 2
♢ A 7 6 3
♣ 9 8 6 2

West	North	East	South
		Pass	Pass
1♠	Pass	2♣	Pass
2♡	Pass	4♠	All Pass

(6)
♠ K 8 5
♡ 7
♢ 6 3
♣ A Q 7 6 5 4 3

♠ J 9 7 4 2
♡ A K 10 5
♢ A 8 2
♣ 2

West	North	East	South
		1♠	
3♣	Pass	3NT	Pass
4♠	All Pass		

(4)   ♠ 8 7 3   ♠ K Q 5 4 2

           ♡ K J 10 6   ♡ 8

           ◇ K 2   **N**   ◇ Q J 10 5

           ♣ K Q J 4   **W E**   ♣ A 10 3

                           S

West	North	East	South
1♣	Pass	1♠	2♡
Dble	Pass	4♠	All Pass

West should have passed the 2♡ overcall. There is no compulsion to double just because you have three-card support. Imagine that East held a weaker hand with only four spades. Then East-West would have had to play in 2♠ rather than defend 2♡, which must be wrong.

Here East's jump to 4♠ was fine. Although West's double did not show any extras, he had the right to expect a more suitable hand for playing in spades.

On the two combined hands above the best game contract is 3NT, but that is very hard to bid. At most vulnerabilities the best East-West score is likely to come from defending 2♡ doubled.

Correct auction:

West	North	East	South
1♣	Pass	1♠	2♡
Pass	Pass	Dble	All Pass

(5) ♠ K 10 9 4 3   ♠ Q J 7
     ♡ Q 10 5 4   ♡ A 2
     ◇ K 2   ◇ A 7 6 3
     ♣ K 4   ♣ 9 8 6 2

West	North	East	South
		Pass	Pass
1♠	Pass	2♣	Pass
2♡	Pass	4♠	All Pass

It looks to me as if West had forgotten he was playing Drury. Or maybe he had not noticed that his partner had already passed (you need to watch for this if you decide to take up Drury). Although some (including me) would open the West hand in any position at the table, it really is nothing to be proud of and game is virtually impossible facing a passed partner. West should sign off in 2♠ over 2♣, showing a sub-minimum opening.

His actual choice of 2♡ led East to believe that he should bid game because not only was he completely maximum for his previous pass, his doubleton heart looked good too.

Correct auction:

West	North	East	South
		Pass	Pass
1♠	Pass	2♣	Pass
2♠	All Pass		

(6)

	♠ K 8 5		♠ J 9 7 4 2
	♡ 7		♡ A K 10 5
	◇ 6 3		◇ A 8 2
	♣ A Q 7 6 5 4 3		♣ 2

West	North	East	South
		1♠	2♡
3♣	Pass	3NT	Pass
4♠	All Pass		

What went wrong? Absolutely nothing. Although the game reached was a little pushy it would have made in practice.

The trouble is that when this deal turned up I was playing a weak no-trump and four-card majors. When my partner bid 3♣ over 2♡, it seemed absurd to rebid my mouldy five-card spade suit when I had such good stoppers in hearts. But when I rebid 3NT partner did not know that I had five spades. I might have had a strong no-trump with four poor spades and king doubleton of clubs when to remove 3NT to 4♠ would have been ridiculous. So, without either of us doing anything wrong we had managed to bid this pair of hands to the absurd contract of 3NT.

This hand is an excellent example of the advantages of playing five-card majors.